FAITH IN THE ER

Faith in the ER

INSPIRATIONAL TRUE STORIES FROM
AN EMERGENCY ROOM DOCTOR

Douglas D. Brunette, MD

Dedication

This book is dedicated to my patients, their families, and their friends, from whom I have learned so much.

Contents

❧

Prologue

❦

THAT GODDAMNED SUN! IT WAS UNBELIEVABLY BRIGHT and intense, almost to the point of being unbearable. It was 6:00 a.m. On any other day, I might have appreciated its beauty. But certainly not today. *Just my damn luck to be assigned an east-facing room.* The bed was angled directly toward a window that had no shades or blinds. The window was perfectly aligned with the sun. The sun, minutes ago having fully emerged above the horizon, emitted its deeply penetrating light rays. These light rays had a perfect straight-line path from the surface of the sun, approximately ninety-three million miles away, through this solitary bare window and directly into my eyes as my head rested on the pillow. The perfectly clear morning blue sky, without even a trace of clouds, made the whole visual experience at that time of day—on this particular day—absolutely painful. *I just want to sleep.* I wanted to avoid thinking of the events of the past twenty-four hours and the events to come later that day. But it was too late. I was awake, tense, anxious, and pissed off. I started to have a repetitive and extremely negative stream of thoughts that I could not mentally control. I knew, at that moment, sleep would not return, and I was destined to spend the next several hours awake and contemplating my fate.

CHAPTER 1

Formative Years

I WAS BAPTIZED AT A FEW MONTHS of age as a Roman Catholic. My parents were dedicated weekly church service parishioners, strong believers not only in the existence of a God, but literal believers in all the tenets of the Roman Catholic faith. They were not bible pounding and never sought, at least in my presence, to overtly proselytize. Their faith was quiet and unshakable and seemed to strengthen in times of trouble. My parents actively practiced their faith. Not just in terms of attending church every Sunday and each religious holiday, but in how they lived their lives. They treated everyone with respect, regardless of their station in life. In our household, a prayer of grace was recited before each meal. The responsibility to deliver the prayer of grace was rotated and shared with my parents, my two younger brothers, and, of course, myself. When my parents spoke the prayer of grace, they were somehow able to narrate this petition each time as if it was the first time in months they had food to eat! It appeared they were genuinely, deeply, and sincerely grateful for every morsel of food they had at every meal. When it was my duty to recite the blessing for our meals, I would deliver those words in the minimal amount of time required, in a not-so-subtle effort to get it over with and start eating. It was a meaningless ritual to me. The food tasted the same, whether blessed or not.

My parents provided me with great religious role models. They taught me nightly prayers. These prayers were quietly whispered while kneeling at the side of my bed. Most of these prayers centered on being grateful for the presence of a loving family, food, clothing, and a home. I often omitted praying for my brothers, the result of intense sibling rivalry.

It never seemed as though my parents deliberately and knowingly forced religion upon me. To them, religion, God, and prayer were as integral to life as breathing. It was taken for granted, an a priori, that their children would follow in their religious footsteps. As time went on, I am afraid I disappointed them in this regard.

I attended a Roman Catholic elementary school. It was archetypal of Roman Catholic grade schools in the early 1960s. The mandatory uniforms for boys consisted of light gray, heavy wool pants and white, long-sleeve dress shirts with a wide plaid tie and uncomfortable black dress shoes. The girls had even worse-looking attire requirements. Their mandatory apparel included a disagreeable below-the-knee plaid skirt that matched the boy's ties, a white, short-sleeved shirt buttoned all the way up to their chin, and white stockings falling just short of their knees. Every school day started and ended with a short church service. My teachers were all nuns. I am not sure what their teaching qualifications were for the actual courses being taught. However, many if not most of these teaching nuns possessed an uncanny ability to gain your entire and focused attention on the subject matter at hand. They accomplished this in several ways, with corporal punishment being the most effective weapon in their arsenal. I had an experience in fourth grade, a full fifty-three years ago, that now elicits a chuckle, but at the time was simply terrifying. I was caught misbehaving. The exact nature of this misbehavior has long since been forgotten, perhaps in an unconscious effort to deflect the responsibility for the event away from myself. Sister "AB" was well-known among our parochial school student circles as the meanest nun in our school. It is possible she was the meanest nun in the entire Archdiocese. She was my fourth-grade teacher who discovered the error of my ways and decided I needed some negative reinforcement therapy. In front of my entire fourth-grade class, I had to hold my hands outstretched, palms facing the floor, and endure a hard slap to the back of my hands with a three-foot-long wooden ruler. Physically painful and mentally embarrassing and shameful, I fought back the tears. I slithered back to my desk, all too excruciatingly aware of the twenty sets of fourth-grade student eyes peering at me. I avoided direct eye contact with all my classmates, and I certainly avoided direct eye contact with Sister AB. I spent the rest of that day licking my wounds in a figurative sense. Unfortunately, I doubled down on my misbehaving mistake later that evening. I decided to tell my dad that Sister AB had slapped my hands hard with a wooden ruler. I told my father that it had hurt tremendously, and that she could have broken my fingers or my hand. I was trying to extract some measure of sympathy from my father, perhaps even encourage him to speak to the school principle on my behalf. My dad did not ask the obvious question, that being, "Why did she hit you?" No, he did not ask that question. He did not ask that question because he did not care why she hit me. Do you know what he did say to me? "Son, don't ever tell me again your teacher hit you in school. If she did, it was for your own good, and you deserved it." My father's comment represented an abrupt end to that complaining session. I must admit, though, that the corporal punishment I received at the hands of Sister AB was loaded with strong negative reinforcement and it must have worked. It was the only time in grade school that my behavior was singled out as needing a physical correction.

Nuns were an enigma to me in elementary school. They were so religious and pious while at the same time they were so mean! That was an inconsistency or incongruity that a young mind could not understand. How could these nuns, who dedicated their lives to their God and religion, hit little, defenseless children? Many did not seem to like being around children. Many possessed a very formal approach to education and management of children. It was a "don't speak until spoken to" methodology. This regimented style did not suit my personality, and if it did anything, it fostered the be-ginnings of my internal rebellion against religion. My fourth-grade teacher, Sister AB, was the meanest person I had ever encountered at that point in my young life. She was not the reason I strayed from organized religion, but despite her corporal punishment tactics, she did not steer me back to the pious path, either. Notwithstanding my parents exposing me to a lot of religion early in my life, I just did not fall in line. At this time in my life I was not religious, I was not an atheist, and I was not an agnos-tic. I was not apathetic, nor was I indifferent. I was simply too preoccupied with sports and friends to even think about God and religion. I did not fall into a religious category because I gave it absolutely zero thought. I had no challenges in my life to make me think anything else was important. It just never entered my daily existence or thoughts. When going to church on Sundays with my parents, I would enter an hour-long session of kid medi-tation. I was way before my time. Meditation would not become popular and mainstream for a few more decades. I literally would daydream for the entire hour, having to be periodically elbow nudged by my parents or siblings during the service to stand, sit, or go receive communion at the specified appropriate times.

I am not sure why, but my parents sent me to a public high school. I was as surprised at that decision as anyone. Perhaps they wanted me to experience a more secular school environment. Well, mission accomplished. I experienced the secular high school lifestyle. High school was simply full of fun. It consisted of sports and parties with some intermittent education thrown into the mix. I did well academically, but not by the power of hard work. I did well by the power of being able to cram at the last minute and scratch out good grades. Which makes my decision in junior year of high school to become a physician somewhat mystifying. It takes a lot of hard work, dedication, and planning to become a physician, and so far in my education I had yet to demonstrate the motivation and ability it would take to realize this goal.

Religion continued to take a back seat on my life bus during high school. Again, this was not an active decision. I was just too busy and interested in everything and anything else. Religion and God were just not needed, required, or desired. I went to church on Sundays with my family as it was a parental expectation, and I had enough respect for my parents not to rock the boat. I continued my church daydreaming. The funniest thing about high school and my lack of religious inclination was the interaction I had with my guidance counselor in choosing which colleges to apply for entrance. My counselor was a devout Roman Catholic, and he knew I was Catholic. The initial list of schools he presented to me to which to apply included St. John's, Notre Dame, Georgetown, Holy Cross, Providence, Sacred Heart, Villanova, and Thomas Aquinas! All were Roman Catholic powerhouses! When my dad and mom saw this list, they were pleased, to say the least. In the meantime, I had read about this small, liberal arts university in upstate New York called St. Lawrence University. It caught my attention, maybe because it was a seven-hour drive from home and nestled in the isolated foothills of the Adirondack Mountains. I was enchanted with the romantic idea of living on my own. An isolated university seemed like a good place to foster this notion. St. Lawrence University soon became my number-one choice for admittedly superfluous and inappropriate reasons. My guidance counselor thought it was a great choice, not knowing that it was a nondenominational institution! I kept all the other suggested Catholic-based schools on my list, continuing the charade of wanting to attend a Catholic university, and placed all my eggs in one basket: the St. Lawrence University basket. I was accepted and never did inform my guidance counselor of his misconception.

CHAPTER 2

College

ST. LAWRENCE UNIVERSITY IS A LIBERAL ARTS college that had requirements at the time of my matriculation for its students to attend classes from all the classic educational domains, including the social sciences, literature, language, math, hard sciences, history, arts, and philosophy. My freshman year I took an introduction to philosophy course. Much of the semester was centered on the philosophy of religion and the belief (or not) in the existence of God. I found the topic fascinating. Whether God existed or not was a question I had never raised with myself. My upbringing initially made the answer to this question a no-brainer. Of course there was a God. It was formal religion that I had not found a use for yet. My professor, an aging and prototypic liberal university professor, was a devout atheist. I know, "devout atheist" sounds like an oxymoron. This well-educated, erudite, fatherly figure who garnered the respect of his students helped change the shape of my religious thinking. Up to this point in my life, I had been a willing participant in religious activity for the sake of conformity and family unity. I had spent little time thinking about what I believed. This philosophy course forced me to contemplate the existence of God. I was required to write in essays my personal thoughts and ideas. In doing so, I began to question myself. I was not an atheist at this moment in my life, but I was becoming an agnostic. I became convinced that there simply was no evidence for or against the existence of a God, at least evidence that I was willing in which to place my trust. My physics courses contributed to my agnostic beliefs. It seemed to me at the time that an omnipotent God would have a better way to start things off than with a "big bang" followed by billions of years of universe development and the subsequent evolution of life. Creationism certainly fulfills the notion of God producing a world in grand and majestic fashion. Creationism, however, is contradicted by all scientific data clearly delineating the evolution of the physical universe as well as Earth life. The late, great, Steven Hawking, one of the premier physics scientists that has ever lived, believed that science and the laws of physics and nature precluded the existence of a God. If there was no tangible scientific evidence for or against the presence of a God, why waste your time in religious matters? Why even ask the question? No one has the answer, no matter how vociferous the argument. College started and fostered my deliberate turn away not only from organized religion, but from a belief in God as well.

I was premed with a firm commitment to become a physician. I soon discovered that I could not get away with the poor study habits I had developed in high school. I was going to have to apply myself. College was a very self-centered time in my life. I had no responsibilities to anyone except to myself. I focused on getting good grades, partying with friends, and sports. I was so engrossed in "me"—my friends, my grades, my fun, my, my, my—there was no religion in my life. I never went to church. That's not a true statement. While home for the holidays, I went to church on Christmas as part of my continued respect for my parents, and not for any other reason. I graduated from college, was accepted into medical school, and began another chapter in my life that not only sharpened my agnostic beliefs but started me thinking there may indeed not be a God.

One last reflection on this time in my life: It became apparent to me that a person did not have to go to church in order to be a moral and ethical individual. I had a strong moral compass. I believed in right and wrong, sometimes to a black-and-white fault. This observation started very close to home. My father and his brother were extremely emotionally close. They owned and worked together in the same family business, and our families lived within three hundred yards of each other for twenty-two years, including from the time I was born until I left for college. My uncle was also my godfather and was very much a second father figure to me. He was kind, personable, and jovial. He was loyal to his family and friends, and he would give you the shirt off his back if you asked. I admired him intensely. At some point it dawned on me that he hardly ever went to church, unlike my father. I never bothered to ask him why. I really don't know what he thought of Catholicism, other religions, or God. Maybe I was justifying being an agnostic, but I distinctly remember thinking that not being religious in the classic sense does not mean you are incapable of a worthy and meaning-filled life, like my uncle's life.

CHAPTER 3

Medical School

I WAS VERY FORTUNATE TO ATTEND VANDERBILT University School of Medicine. It is a well-respected medical institution known for its academic excellence in research, education, and delivery of medical care. I do not know what it is like to attend medical school now, but I do remember with vivid detail what it was like for me back then. Eight hours per day in either a classroom or a laboratory for the first two years. Human anatomy, physiology, microbiology, molecular biology, pathology, pharmacology, and histology filled my days. Day in and day out, I was bombarded by facts, data, and medical theories. I quickly became a human scientist entrenched in the study of human functioning. The complexities of the human condition and existence were unraveled in detailed, scientific analysis. Human physiologic phenomena that seemed before medical school to be "miraculous" were readily explained using scientific inquiry. The exquisite and exact matching of form and function and human anatomy and its purpose was quickly accepted as a matter of natural fact. Fractured bones, for example, healed due to the interaction of various cells and hormones in the human body that could be fully explained on a molecular level. This was a complex process broken down into understandable, finite, and discrete scientific facts and principles. Nature, not God, explained these complex processes. The mysteries of nature that were not yet fully understood as a result of scientific inquiry would eventually become known by scientific advancement. It would only be a matter of time for medical discoveries to fill in current knowledge deficiencies. God was not needed to explain the unknown in terms of human function. Only more scientific and medical research was needed. This abandonment of the need for God to explain the unknown has a long history not limited to medicine. Gods once responsible for fire, thunder, oceans, heavenly objects, and indeed, life itself, have been discarded once scientific inquiry discovered the factual and tangible reasons these phenomena exist. The same is true of complex human anatomy, physiology, and pathology.

The second two years of medical school are clinical, meaning students spend six to eight weeks rotating on various medical specialties such as internal medicine, surgery, pediatrics, psychiatry, and emergency medicine. Long days were the routine, and nights on call occurred all too often. It was the beginning of applying newfound book knowledge to the practice of medicine. It was the first time I had been really exposed to illness, injury, human tragedy, and death. My scientific training took precedence in how I approached these emotionally difficult encounters. I learned to explain every illness, every injury, and every tragedy in cold, ruthless scientific terms. It is possible that my reaction to this was self-protective. It was way easier to face illness, injury, and human tragedy with a calculating scientific mindset than to expose your vulnerable and emotional underbelly.

My medical school years furthered my agnostic beliefs. I studied in detail the inner workings of the most complex contraption that existed on Earth (i.e., the human body). I had scientific answers as to why and how things happened to patients and was beginning to learn what to do about it. God continued to be nonexistent for me. There was no need for him (her) in my life. There were scientific reasons why illness, accident, and human tragedy occurred. If there were gaps in knowledge of the human condition, well, it was only a matter of time before those gaps were filled in by scientific pursuit.

Despite all the education in medical school, you are never really placed in a position of authority or decision-making in providing medical care to patients. Someone your senior is almost always at your side, guiding you in whatever medical care you are being taught to provide. In a way, you are protected from the hard responsibilities of tending to the sick. If something does not go according to plan, the medical student was not to blame. In a way I found myself, like in college, accountable only to myself and my education and free of any real responsibilities.

I continued to focus on myself, my education, and not much else.

CHAPTER 4

Internship and Residency

AFTER GRADUATING FROM MEDICAL SCHOOL, I DECIDED to specialize in emergency medicine and spend my career working as an emergency physician. I did not characterize myself as an adrenaline junkie at the time. It was the extreme variety of patients and pathology and the ability to perform procedures, some of them lifesaving, that was alluring. In choosing this specialty, I thought that I would never get bored. In the end, I was correct. At times I became tired, but I was never bored.

Residency training in the specialty of emergency medicine is rigorous. It is demanding intellectually, emotionally, and physically. It is three to four years long, and is composed of a gradual, but very definitive, progression of increasing clinical responsibility. Although physician mentors (i.e., teaching faculty) are readily available, nonetheless as a resident in training you make decisions that affect patients' lives. Indeed, at times, life-and-death decisions were made. I clearly remember moments of intense anxiety, even fear, when faced with life-and-death scenarios. I learned to suppress and ignore those feelings.

I learned to think clearly despite the intense emotional circumstances. As an example, a patient once presented with a self-inflicted gunshot wound to the face. Despite his face being grotesquely distorted and unrecognizable, he was alive. My teaching faculty instructed me to focus solely on getting a breathing tube in the patient's trachea (windpipe). But how? I cannot find his nose, mouth, or tongue, and air is bubbling up from the mangled facial tissue. Right now, nothing else in the world matters to me except placing a breathing tube in this poor man's trachea. Per my teaching faculty, that is all that is important. This is but one admittedly extreme example of how intense training in emergency medicine teaches you to not react emotionally. You are there to do a job. Taking the emotions out of the equation at the time of action makes you a better physician. At least that is what we were taught. Religion, and a belief in God, never entered my mind in these times of crisis. I never prayed for my patients or their families. I felt deep sympathy and empathy for them. And I hoped things turned out well for them. But I never prayed for them. I also never asked for God to make me a better physician or to help me with a difficult patient case.

I discovered how capricious and seemingly unfair life could be. I was exposed to horrible events in my patients' and in their families' lives. I witnessed lives being forever changed in an instant from just being in the wrong place at the wrong time. The examples are too numerous to count. A crash caused by a drunk driver. A large tree falling in a storm, crushing victims as they walked on an adjacent path. A tire falling off a truck traveling at seventy miles per hour, striking the windshield of a trailing car. A deer bounding onto a highway, causing a severe head-on collision. House fires and explosions, accidental falls from heights or just on slippery ice, accidental firearm injury, work-related events such as electrical injury and farm equipment mishaps. It seemed like every day something bad happened to someone, many times through no fault of their own, that radically and permanently altered their life. I was a witness to this daily mayhem.

Along these same lines, I witnessed the terrible things that humans perpetrate on other humans. Blunt force assaults, stab wounds, and gunshot injuries. Domestic violence, physical and sexual pediatric assault, and road-rage crashes. There were also the unfortunately common self-inflicted injuries such as hangings, gunshot wounds, and toxic ingestions.

The sum response of my residency training as it affected my religious beliefs was straightforward. I started to believe that there was absolutely no rhyme or reason for many events in life. It was just a crapshoot. I questioned how any God could stand by and watch this human suffering. I went from being an agnostic, and neither denying nor accepting the existence of God, to being really pissed off at his (her) reluctance to intervene. Eventually, this anger at God gave way to a belief that there was no God.

Occam's Razor[1] is a scientific principle that I have found to be quite beneficial in my work as a physician. This principle can be summed up with the following statement: the simplest explanation that accounts for all the observed facts and data is likely to be the correct explanation. Correctly diagnosing patient illness can be, at times, quite difficult, especially when confronted with competing or confusing facts. Occam's razor is especially beneficial in determining the correct patient diagnosis. Applying Occam's razor to medical diagnostic evaluation proved to be quite advantageous for me. It is not universally accurate, as in medicine there are sometimes complex diagnostic answers that cannot be simplified. After all, a patient can have two separate and unrelated diagnoses contributing to their current and complex illness.

I found myself applying Occam's razor to answer this troubling God notion in my mind at this point in my life. Why would a God, by definition capable of doing anything, allow for the daily onslaught of human suffering that frequently unfolded itself to me? God as described in many of the great religions of the world was a force with unlimited power and capability. Nothing was beyond his (her) reach and capacity. Yet it seemed that if there was a God, he (she) was indifferent toward the human plight. Instead, Occam's razor allowed me to conclude, in simple fashion, that there was no God. This would be a much simpler explanation of the witnessed

---

1 https://en.wikipedia.org/wiki/Occam%27s_razor

facts of life on Earth. I came to believe the physicists like Steven Hawking were likely correct. The big bang was not a result of an act of God, but rather a spontaneous event fully explained by the laws of physics. Nothing, including time itself, existed prior to the big bang. Time and everything that occurred subsequent to the big bang was driven by the laws of physics.

CHAPTER 5

My Own Family

I MARRIED IN 1983. MY WIFE CAME from a large, German, Roman Catholic farming family. They were hardworking, salt of the earth people and were devoted to their family and to God. Her hometown of six hundred people, like so many small towns in rural Minnesota, had the requisite bank, small grocery store, gas station, post office, a couple of bars, and a church. The church was the largest structure for miles. It was disproportionately outsized compared to the rest of the buildings in town. It bordered on opulence, having beautiful, expansive stained-glass windows, intricate wooden artwork carvings, and a huge marble altar. It clearly cost a boatload of money to erect. I often wondered where the money came from to build such an impressive church. I would not have thought that a small farming town with a population of six hundred could afford to build such a structure.

My wife and I started a family in 1991. As with most new parents, the presence of children changed our lives dramatically. We were no longer living just for ourselves. We now had the added important responsibility of raising children. At first the responsibility appeared daunting. You would not think that an emergency physician faced with life-and-death decisions almost every day would feel the heat of responsibility that comes with raising children. But I did. In the beginning, every decision concerning our children seemed major! Fortunately, as time went on, I learned to relax.

I was determined to raise my kids to be respectful, moral, and ethical individuals. I did not think I needed religion to accomplish this goal. But my wife did. She never wavered in her religious beliefs, and she was quite determined to raise our children with a proper Roman Catholic upbringing. It was never a source of contention between us. We both wanted the same result for our children. We just had different ideas about how to get them there when it came to religion. So we baptized them, and I watched them receive their First Communion followed by their Confirmation. I was there every step of the way physically, but not so much mentally. I supported my wife and kids in these endeavors, but I never really bought into the importance of religious ceremony. I had a personal saying in those days that reflected well my thinking at the time. I kept this private saying confidential, sharing it with no one: *God may or may not have invented man, but man definitely invented religion.*

The late 1980s saw the first scattered reports of Roman Catholic priests involved in sexual abuse. The 1990s is when large exposes on Roman Catholic priests as sexual predators began to surface. We had two young children in the 1990s, and the reports of sexual exploitation of young children by priests really hit a nerve with me. These were priests who were supposedly religious, dedicating their life to their God, and yet preyed on innocent children. It was another justification for my negative impression and feelings for organized religion. I personally knew people who never went to church but who led exemplary moral lives (like my uncle, for one). Others, like the priests who preyed on innocent children, had the external appearance of piety but clearly were deplorable on the inside. I would look at my own kids and just shake my head. Why would this happen? Why would God let this happen? How could priests do this? How could other priests, the administrators of the church, cover it up? These are questions that go unanswered for me to this day. Again, I applied Occam's razor. There was no God.

CHAPTER 6

Early to Middle Adulthood

I SPENT THE NEXT COUPLE OF DECADES of my life kind of on autopilot. I had only sporadic and trivial health issues. I was happily married to a wonderful person and had two kids that were intelligent and successful in the classroom. Both of our children were athletically inclined, and my wife and I spent a good portion of our awake and nonworking time at a skating rink, gym, or golf course watching and supporting our kids' sports activities. I had a great job as an academic emergency medicine physician at a teaching hospital, and the work, centered on patient care, teaching, and research, was extremely rewarding. The only significant stress I endured during this time period surrounded the deaths of my parents. The loss of parents is always a milestone in one's life. Although it was difficult to experience, my life as an emergency medicine physician had helped prepare me for this personal loss. I had seen the circle of life innumerable times in my physician role, and I knew that one day it would happen to me.

My involvement in religion during this time period was limited to attending church services on Christmas, Easter, memorials, and the official Catholic rites of passage for my children, such as First Communion and Confirmation. Involvement is probably too strong a word, as it implies that I spiritually participated, contributed, and felt connected to the religious ceremony, which certainly was not the case. I never dissented in physically participating and did my best to participate meaningfully, but it was never an important part of my life. I did not pray for anyone or anything. The closest I came to prayer was to silently wish for someone to have a good outcome in whatever tribulation they might be enduring. But I never connected that wish to religion or a God.

During this time period, I continued to witness innumerable tragedies in my daily work as an emergency medicine physician. I was steadfast in my belief that there was no God. Even if I was wrong, it was clear to me that God was a big-time underperformer. I would frequently find myself just shaking my head, wondering why such a terrible event would happen. What purpose does tragedy serve in a universe created by a supreme being who, according to most religions, is loving, kind, all-knowing, and forgiving? It is a question that has been asked by humans for as long as humans have existed, and we are no closer to knowing the answer than when we first started asking the question. People of strong faith typically answer that question with "I don't know why tragedy, pain,

and suffering exist, but God does." That answer was never adequate for me. It did not provide one ounce of satis-
faction, comfort, or confidence.

So I traveled through these years without a personal
connection to religion or to a God. In fact, I cultivated
animosity toward both. In terms of God, I just could not
reconcile the seemingly endless pain and suffering I
witnessed daily with a benevolent, all-knowing, and all-
loving God. It just did not make any teleological sense.
Formal religion to me was even more of an issue. It
seemed to me that formal religions were created by man
and often abused by man. The study of human history
is replete with religious wars and human suffering related to differences of religious belief. The sexual assault
abuse of young male children by Roman Catholic priests
was particularly emotionally disturbing to me. So I lived
as moral a life as I could during this time period, raising
my children in the same fashion, and emotionally and
mentally ditched God and religion.

CHAPTER 7

My Life-Threatening
Medical Emergency

I AM FIFTY-FOUR YEARS OLD. I HAVE just been admitted to the hospital after having significant chest pain while riding an exercise bike at the gym the previous day. I immediately knew this chest pain was emanating from my heart. The symptom is called angina, and it is a stern warning of an impending heart attack. This pain was different than any other chest pain I had ever experienced in my life. After listening to hundreds of patients describe these symptoms, the etiology of my pain was unmistakable. Yet denial is a strong protective mechanism *Homo sapiens* has. It took me a day to accept my plight and agree with my wife to go get checked out. The cardiologist performed a physical examination, and on the outside, I appeared quite physically fit. An electrocardiogram (EKG) and blood tests revealed no evidence of a heart attack. I began to think I had overreacted to some stomach indigestion as there was no evidence yet of a cardiac problem. For my last test, I was placed on a medical exercise treadmill for cardiac testing in the late afternoon. This test was short-lived. After only one minute, I developed the same, heavy, distressing, squeezing, and enveloping chest pain I had experienced while on the exercise bike the day before. I quickly got off the medical treadmill, laid flat on an adjacent examination table, and the cardiologist immediately performed a cardiac ultrasound test. This ultrasound test enabled the cardiologist to directly view how well my heart was working. It took him just a few seconds of viewing and assessing my abnormal heart contraction movement before he muttered, much too loudly for my sense of taste, "Oh shit." I might add this spontaneous and uninhibited verbal proclamation by my cardiologist in response to the appearance of my grossly abnormal exercise cardiac ultrasound test demonstrated a very poor bedside manner. I wondered at the time if he muttered "Oh shit" every time he saw an abnormal stress cardiac ultrasound. I hoped not. Being an emergency medicine physician, though, I understood and could appreciate his forthright reaction. Patients not in the medical field probably would not welcome his frankness. After a few very anxious minutes, my chest pain resolved. I was immediately given 325 mg of aspirin to help prevent blood clotting and a heart attack. I suddenly realized that my schedule for the next several days had just been drastically altered. I was not anticipating what other radical effects this event was about to bestow upon me, not only physically, but mentally and spiritually. It was early evening by the time I was admitted to my hospital room. I attempted to distract myself with a combination of reading, television, and visiting with my immediate family. Once visiting hours were over, I endeavored to settle down and relax. The uncomfortable bed and pillow, and the almost constant intrusive noise of a busy hospital ward, made the onset of sleep difficult. It was well after midnight when sleep finally overcame me. I had expended a significant amount of nervous energy during the past twenty-four hours, and the physiologic necessity for sleep finally overwhelmed my continued anxiety.

The following morning, I was awakened by that "goddamned sun." A few hours after awakening, I was in a cardiac catheterization lab. The procedure involved poking a needle into the femoral artery in my groin, placing a long catheter and wire into my femoral artery and moving it two feet northbound through my aorta and into my coronary (heart) arteries. The coronary arteries supply blood to the heart itself. By injecting contrast dye into the coronary arteries while continuous x-rays are taken, the coronary arteries are examined to see if they have a blockage causing the symptoms. In my case, 95 percent of my left anterior descending coronary artery was occluded or blocked from severe atherosclerosis, otherwise known as hardening of the arteries. This coronary artery supplies blood to a very large portion of the heart, and its complete occlusion could easily result in instant death. My level of sedation waxed and waned during the cardiac procedure. During a period of the procedure when I was relatively awake, I distinctly remember my interventional cardiologist telling me as he examined my coronary arteries on the computer screen that he had found my problem. I also distinctly remember responding to his proclamation by retorting rudely "Stop talking and get it fixed." Which he promptly did by placing a permanent stent across my diseased coronary artery. This stent held my diseased coronary artery wide open, thus permitting normal blood flow to my heart muscle. As it turns out, I had just a single lesion in all my coronary arteries, and that lesion was now permanently fixed. I spent one additional night in the hospital and was discharged the following morning.

It's now two days after discharge from the hospital. Modern medicine is impressive. Two days prior a stent was placed in my diseased coronary artery, fixing a potentially life-threatening lesion. It is hard to imagine that a small blockage, one-eighth the size of my little fingernail, could have resulted in my sudden death.

Now I'm standing at my garage workbench at home, tinkering with repairing a piece of equipment. I had been given specific doctors' orders to slowly increase my level of activity. I thought playing with some light workbench equipment was perfectly fine. I love to do projects around the house, both big and small. Dismantle, build, fix, and improve. It always provided a much-needed distraction for me when the pressures of emergency medicine mounted. Much to my wife's chagrin, I often tackled household undertakings with little practical knowledge. I would google for do-it-yourself videos, gathering the knowledge I needed and then proceed to take on the household task. I would purchase or rent the needed equipment, buy the supplies, and wade right in. It did not matter to me that I had never done something before. Not having done something before was actually enticing, rewarding, and part of the fun. This approach, as you could imagine, often resulted in some initial failures. For example, there is a big difference in watching a YouTube video on grinding a concrete floor with a high-speed diamond grinder and doing it yourself! That piece of equipment almost flew uncontrollably through the closed garage door when I first turned it on!

I had developed a habit (yes, a bad habit) years prior of cursing when struggling and failing to do a difficult task. I had a large repertoire of expletive-deleted phrases when frustrated with a project. However, "goddamn it" was my favorite phrase. Somehow it made me feel better, and I had a perverse notion that somehow saying "goddamn it" would help in the resolution of whatever task I was failing to perform. "Goddamn it" spewed out of my mouth when that concrete grinder flew out of my hands! There exists scientific evidence indicating there are mental health benefits of cursing, but I will save that for another time.

My lightweight workbench tinkering was a great way to pass some time. It would be several days before being cleared to go back to work and full physical activity. The task at hand appeared simple. I needed to place a small piece of copper pipe onto a form-fitting metal flange. What started off as a modest task soon became a source of immense frustration. It just would not connect, despite my knowing it was the correct size and shape and that it should fit. I tried different angles of approach, switched hands, and lubricated the pieces meant to attach to each other. No luck. I rested for a few minutes in between failed attempts. I finally did what I was specifically instructed not to do by my cardiologist (i.e., exert myself). I took a deep breath and applied significant force to position the pipe onto the metal flange. Still no success. Emergency medicine physicians are known for their short attention span, and the short period of time from when frustration develops to a call for action. Sometimes any action is better than no action. I am no different. After what seemed to be an innumerable number of attempts over a prolonged time period, my frustration grew and grew. However, this prolonged time period was only a few short minutes.

Here is the where things got interesting. This is the exact type of situation that would warrant my cursing. At this point in my ever-increasing frustration, normally the thought to verbalize out loud the words "goddamn it" would originate in my brain's language center. This would then be followed immediately by my lips and larynx collaborating, carrying out the brain's command, and yelling out that exact curse. But that's not what happened. For some reason, my brain's language center did not conjure up "goddamn it" as it had done so many thousands of times before in my life. Instead, the specific thought I had was a question: "*God, can you help me here?*" I had *never* had that thought before in my entire life—not even in times of intense stress; not even during deeply personal events that were much more anxiety-provoking. I had lost my parents just a couple of years prior to this event, and I never had the inclination to ask God for his help during that emotional time period of my life. To this very day, I have absolutely no idea why this thought and question popped into my head. Its origin remains a complete and total enigma to me. At this point in my life I was an atheist, and a plea to a God that I did not believe existed was self-contradictory. It was also quite weird to have my very first plea to God in my fifty-four-year-old life be a request to help me in such a menial and unimportant task. Where the hell did that thought come from?

However, what I do know is that it was not a real plea. I was not really asking God for help. I was being sarcastic. I can still feel the disparaging tone that enveloped that question, my emotional feeling as I thought the question was cynical, mocking, and acerbic. I did not have the slightest inclination or belief that there was a God watching me struggle with this menial task. Why would there be? No, this was a derisive thought, initiated by a superficial irritation related to the failure of a simple task and contained serious deep undertones of anger, antagonism, and perhaps rage at God's failure to prevent tragedy, or near tragedy, like my coronary artery blockage.

I am not equating failure to place a pipe onto a metal flange as a tragedy. Not at all. But I think this sarcastic thought was, in fact, emblematic of my feelings about the dubious presence of a God. And I cannot help but think that my cardiac events of the past week, together with my selfishness, played a role in this response.

Despite the command from my brain's language center to mutter out loud the sarcastic question, the words asking for help were never actually vocalized into sound. I never actually physically voiced the question for God's help. That's because there was not enough time. Less than a nanosecond after having the thought of the sardonic question, but before I had any time to verbalize the question on my lips, THE PIPE SLID NICELY AND SECURELY OVER THE METAL FLANGE! The mental question and the securing of the pipe were almost instantaneous events. The action of the pipe slipping over the flange was not rough and was not associated with any strenuous mechanical action. It slipped, as in glided, slid, or slithered. It went on smoothly, almost without effort, in direct contrast to the twenty or so other unsuccessful attempts immediately preceding the successful effort. I stumbled backward as a result of being mentally stunned. My question seemed to have been rapidly answered in the affirmative. "Yes, I can help you." Was this really an answer?

Or was it a coincidence? A fortuitous event? Just plain chance? Perhaps. That would have been my answer in the past. I would have explained away the event. But I did not brush it off. I could not ignore it. It hit me like a ton of bricks. Here is literally the first time in my entire life I asked for God's help, even if done in a satirical and nonbelieving tone, to do a meaningless and uninspiring task, and I got the help I needed so fast it was overwhelming. I did not even have time for my lips and larynx to produce a single sound. *Are you kidding me?* I sat back and just contemplated the event again. *What just happened to me?*

What in the world...

It had been an emotional and stressful week for me. Two days ago, I faced my own mortality in a cardiac catheterization lab. I knew that many people just drop dead from the exact cardiac lesion I had, having not being given the warning signs I had been afforded. I sat thinking about the past week's events. I recalled looking at my wife's face as I was being rolled into the cardiac catheterization lab. Without speaking, her countenance relayed several messages. These included "I am here for you and I will be waiting for you," "Don't you dare die on me," "You are scaring the hell out of me," and "I feel helpless." I recollected calling my kids and letting them know what was happening. Over the phone they just froze, being completely taken aback by the bad news. I knew as I was being wheeled into the cardiac catheterization lab that I had coronary artery disease. I just did not know the extent of the cardiac disease. I knew the odds were good that I would awaken from my sedation and whatever procedure was performed. But I also knew, as I have witnessed patients in the past, that I could have a major complication with morbidity or even mortality. It was an emotional roller coaster of a week. I went from being completely healthy, to having a potentially life-threatening event, and back to being completely healthy with disaster averted, all within a twenty-four-hour time period. I now had a wide-open garden hose for a left anterior descending coronary artery, where blood could flow freely to my heart. No more worries about clogging that large conduit. It was time to resume the same old life. Now this weird thing occurs to me.

I sat down on the garage floor. I contemplated this fluke of fitting a pipe onto a metal flange at the exact same time I sardonically asked God for help. I continued to review my past week in detail. It was one traumatic week. In my retrospective review of these past several days, the thought of that sunrise while I tried to sleep in my hospital bed while awaiting my trip to the cardiac catheterization lab bolted into my mind.

That's when my epiphany occurred. At first this epiphany was rather disconcerting. That sunrise was not a painful, arbitrary, capricious happenstance that occurred just by the luck of the draw in being assigned to that hospital room with the perfectly aligned window aimed at the sun. The thought occurred to me that the sunrise was a sign telling me everything was going to be fine. It's just that I did not realize it at the time. All I knew was that the sun was painful and incredibly irritating. I did not see how beautiful the sunrise was, nor appreciate its metaphorical significance as it related to my current predicament. Sunrises have long been associated with feelings of promise, optimism, and hope. Dawn of a new day brings aspirations, possibilities, and confidence.

Yet I reacted to my sunrise two days ago with anger, annoyance, and irritation. As I recalled that sunrise in this new light (pardon the pun), I felt sheepish, uncomfortable, and perhaps a bit ashamed. I felt small.

Now, it's two days later, and perhaps another, maybe not-so-subtle sign was just sent to me. Two compelling instances in two days, revolving around a very emotional and sensitive life event.

My description and emotional reaction to these signs might appear to the reader as melodramatic, sensational, overemotional, and exaggerated. Perhaps over the top, histrionic, or theatrical are better descriptions. But those are the events that happened to me, and this is how I reacted to them. Pure, simple, and unadulterated.

Several questions roared into my head. Were those really signs? If they were signs, were they really sent to me? Or were they happenstance phenomena that I falsely read into and developed a factitious storyline? Was I assigning a reason or purpose to these events? Was I instilling a story or meaning into them that was fabricated by the cerebral frontal cortex of my brain? Yes, I was exhibiting scientific thinking again.

In the years leading up to this event, I would not have given any credence to these signs. I would have looked upon them as just natural phenomena or coincidence and went about my business. However, the events of this week seemed to make me vulnerable to outside-the-box thinking. For whatever reason, I was suddenly and inexplicably open to alternative thinking.

If they were sent to me, it would logically imply that someone or something sent them. Who, or what, could that force be? The answer was obvious, and very unsettling, if I truly believed they were signs. There really is only one answer.

A Higher Power[2] sent them. Did I immediately become a bible-pounding religious zealot as a result of these signs? No, I did not. Did I suddenly fervently believe, without hesitation, that God was looking down on me? The answer was no. I had spent years ignoring, hiding from, and disavowing any God. Those nonbelieving thoughts were a thick and heavy layer of self-protection and would not be easily removed by a couple of seemingly chance events. But I did think about the possibility of a Higher Power, some force much bigger than my existence, and this thought was strangely comforting.

---

2 The reader will notice that I switched from using the term God to Higher Power. This is a deliberate change due to purely personal choice. Historically for me, the term God rendered specific imagery and personality characteristics which were probably leftover vestiges from my Roman Catholic upbringing. In fact, personification was at the root of my vision of God. He was white, male, grandfatherly, gray haired with a matching beard. His face evoked wisdom, trust and fear, all at the same time. After my transformative life event, the term "God" seemed restrictive and narrow. Throughout all the following narratives in this book, the term "Higher Power" connotes a more flexible, wider-ranging description for God that is more encompassing. There are many names for God used by humans the world over. Each name may elicit different pictures or characteristics of God depending on the specific religion and culture in which the name is being utilized. I use Higher Power from an all-inclusive viewpoint that is not specific to any one religion or culture.

I still did not think about being religious. Religion remained a mechanism for humans to connect with their Higher Power, and the world's vast assortment of differing religions, or customs, if you will, demonstrated the multitude of ways this connection can occur. But for the first time in my life, I felt connected.

I know what some nonbelievers who are reading this passage might be thinking. There are no atheists in foxholes. In other words, the threat of death earlier in the week had altered my thinking and highlighted my need of getting into a better relationship with my Higher Power. After all, why take a chance on there being a hell in the event of my death? But that is not how it happened. I did not bargain with my Higher Power earlier in the week. When I was in the hospital, before being wheeled into the cardiac catheterization laboratory, I did not try to make a deal with my Higher Power, along the lines of "OK, get me through this and I will change my life." Although the thought of potentially dying obviously crossed my mind, the thought of a Higher Power never did. I remained steadfast in my nonrelationship with and nonbelief in a Higher Power, even as I was being wheeled into the cardiac catheterization lab.

Now, suddenly I found myself looking into a metaphorical mirror. I had a really important decision to make. I could ascribe both the sunrise the morning of my cardiac catheterization and the pipe-over-a-flange incident two days later to random occurrences that were dictated by the laws of nature or the laws of physics. This is what I had been doing for most of my adult life. It made the most sense and agreed with and was supported by my scientific training. By doing so, I could continue to not believe in the existence of a Higher Power. This would be the status quo, which is often the easiest choice for humans to make. It certainly would have been the easiest choice for me. I had a fully developed, time-honored sense of self that had long ago removed any Higher Power from my life. I was happy, successful, fulfilled, and led what I thought had been a moral life, all without the belief in a Higher Power. Or I could seriously entertain the opposite. Notably, these were not random events as the result of the laws of nature, but were indeed related to the presence of a Higher Power that for some inexplicable reason decided to materialize himself (herself) in a weird and circuitous manner. Why not just appear in front of me in some ghostly, surreal, frightening fashion to get your point across?

CHAPTER 8

A Jump into Faith

THE NEXT FEW DAYS I THOUGHT OF nothing else. I was totally consumed. I was aloof to my surroundings. I kept asking myself over and over: *Were those two events actually signs sent from a Higher Power?* I found myself at the edge of a metaphorical cliff. I had two choices. My first choice was to step backward from the cliff, turn and walk away, and continue my life and my nonbelief as it existed. It had worked for my first fifty-four years, and there was no reason to believe it would not continue to work for me. Or I could jump. Make the leap of faith. Place enough trust and conviction that these two events were hints from my Higher Power. They were not random, but rather these two events were prescribed specifically for me. What should I do? What did I do?

I jumped.

Free-falling can be scary. This was not. Free-falling from a significant height means you are going to die if you are not caught. The second I jumped, I was caught. There was no trepidation and no anxiety. I felt safe.

The result of the two events—in my mind, unmistakable hints from a Higher Power—was draconian. The walls that I spent years building around me, ignoring, and even denying the existence of a Higher Power came crashing down at my feet. I could not get this out of my mind. It set the stage for this book.

What other signs had I missed over my first fifty-four years of living? I had been an emergency physician for twenty-eight years at this point in my life. All of my career was spent working in an urban, level 1 trauma center caring for those less fortunate. There was virtually nothing in the human condition that I had not either seen and witnessed personally or heard about from colleagues. Then I had the thought that was the genesis of this book. Perhaps previous signs from my Higher Power had been coming my way through my patients and my experiences as an emergency physician. The trouble up to this point in my life was that I was too self-centered and busy with the scientific part of medicine to ever take notice. I was too busy being a doctor, too focused on my job and my responsibilities. I had tunnel vision. I was too absorbed in finding the clinical problem, fixing the clinical problem and moving on to the next patient. An emergency medicine physician in a busy, academic medical center sees a lot of patients over their career. A conservative estimate would be fifty thousand separate patient encounters. I frantically began to recollect many of my myriad patient encounters. Obviously, I could not recall all of my patient interactions, but there are some that clearly stood out for one reason or another. I started to recall the more memorable patients and events. Had they provided me with signs that I failed to recognize? The more patients I recalled, the more convinced I became that there was something to this train of thought. There seemed to be messages, previously unrecognized, in my patient encounters. It was real, and it was inspiring. It motivated me to write this book. What follows are humble narratives of some of my patient encounters and other medical experiences that are providing me with reasons to have "Faith in the ER."

Please realize that at the time when these patient encounters and events occurred, I experienced them at merely face-value on a superficial basis. At the time of these events, I made no connection to a Higher Power. But now looking back on these patient interactions that stood out in my mind, there is no doubt that an underlying reason for these encounters exists. Something else was happening here in my recollection of these events, something only now did I notice in retrospect with wide-open eyes and an exposed heart.

—

CHAPTER 9

A Grieving Family

A SEVENTEEN-YEAR-OLD FEMALE PRESENTED TO THE CRITICAL care room in the emergency department after being involved in a severe motor vehicle crash. It was prom night, and the young patient had been with several friends in a car, going back to her home for an after-prom party. The paramedics reported to us that a drunk driver had swerved into their lane and hit their car head-on with tremendous force. The front of their car had collapsed like an accordion. It took the firefighters and paramedics several long minutes to extricate her from the twisted metallic wreckage. She presented to the emergency department stabilization room unconscious with an obvious significant head injury, a very low blood pressure, and extreme difficulty with breathing. Twelve healthcare workers descended upon her as she lay unresponsive on the gurney. Her beautiful prom dress, now covered and soaked in her blood, was cut off with scissors to facilitate physical examination and the various procedures that would undoubtedly need to be performed. These procedures were happening simultaneously, all with the hope of saving this young life. Large-bore intravenous catheters were placed, and the patient was administered intravenous medications that would temporarily chemically paralyze and sedate her. A breathing tube was placed into her throat, and she was placed on a ventilator to control her respiration. A chest tube was inserted into her left chest cavity to treat a punctured and briskly bleeding lung. An ultrasound examination revealed a hemoperitoneum, or severe bleeding into her abdominal cavity, and was likely the result of a serious liver and/or spleen injury. Her blood pressure was critically low as a result of the intra-abdominal hemorrhage. Medications for slowing the hemorrhage and improving her blood pressure were administered. Massive blood transfusions were immediately undertaken to replace the dangerous amount of blood she had clearly lost. Approximately twelve minutes after arrival in the emergency department, after partial stability in her blood pressure and heart rate appeared to have been obtained, she was readied for transport to the operating room in hope of controlling her abdominal and lung hemorrhage. She never made it to the emergency department stabilization room exit doors. Her heart suddenly slowed, and then simply stopped beating. Aggressive further resuscitation attempts over the next hour proved unsuccessful.

After I formally declared and noted the exact time of death, the room became completely silent and still. No one moved. All were either staring directly at this young, beautiful girl, or were staring at the floor. No one made eye contact with each other. This patient had entered our lives a little over an hour ago as a stranger in need, and she was leaving her mark in our minds, souls, and hearts. No one outwardly and overtly cried, but we were all crying on the inside. I had two kids that went to prom just a couple of years prior to this event. It could just as easily be one of my children, or the child of any member of the healthcare team who had unsuccessfully tried to save her life.

After what seemed to be an inordinate amount of time, each of the healthcare workers in that stabilization room slowly, diligently, and silently returned to their duties.

I started debriefing with the involved medical students and resident physicians. I always thought it most valuable to teach immediately following critical patient cases. The goal was to discuss as objectively as possible the actions of the healthcare team and learn from our experiences. What could or should have been done differently? Many times, cases such as these happen so fast that the inexperienced medical student or resident physician in training is unsure as to why things are being done, including the order in which they are being performed. Teaching immediately after a case is completed, when the circumstances are fresh and real, was, in my opinion, invaluable. In this case, the patient likely had devastating abdominal injuries to either her liver, spleen, or a major blood vessel, in addition to her severe head injury. Despite the chance of survival being extremely low with this constellation of injuries, the expectation on the part of emergency physicians is that we can stabilize most patients and give them a fighting chance for their survival. When such a patient dies in front of you, it makes the outcome even more difficult to accept.

In the middle of my teaching debriefing, the charge nurse unobtrusively approached me from behind.

The charge nurse informed me in a low whisper close to my ear that the patient's family was waiting for me in the family waiting room. This is a small room thirty yards from the critical care room, reserved solely for the family members of critically ill or injured patients. My heart sank. Breaking bad news was perhaps the worst part of a job that I otherwise thoroughly enjoyed. I quickly finished my postcase debriefing with the students and resident physicians. I checked my scrubs to make sure blood had not been spilled on them. It is not appropriate to speak with relatives and have their loved one's blood splattered on your scrubs. I walked slowly down the hall toward the family room, trying to gather my thoughts and prepare for the heartbreak I would soon witness. I entered the family waiting room with our chaplain and charge nurse. It was personally supporting to have the chaplain and the charge nurse with me in these situations. I did not feel so alone with their company. The small room was filled with family members and friends. Mom and dad, two younger siblings, and a grandparent were present, along with three friends who were clearly dressed for a high school prom. I always begin family discussions like this by introducing myself and asking for the names and relationships of those in attendance. I want to try and acknowledge the relatives closest to the patient and direct my full attention to them. After the brief introductions, I pulled a chair up, and sat down directly in front of mom and dad who were sitting on a couch. I leaned into them, knowing full well this would be interpreted by them as an ominous sign. I asked them what they knew, if anything, about what happened that night. Many times, families know beforehand the gravity of the situation and are already steadying themselves for the worst news to come out of my mouth. Unfortunately, this was not the case tonight. The parents had little information. All the parents knew was that their treasured daughter had been involved in a car crash and had been taken by ambulance to our hospital. They knew nothing else. It was up to me tell them.

"Your daughter was involved in a major head-on car crash. When she arrived by ambulance, she was unconscious from a severe head injury. She had many internal injuries with significant bleeding and difficulty breathing. We did everything we possibly could do." It was at this very moment that the mom and dad—indeed, everyone in the room—began to weep, anticipating, even knowing what my next words were going to be. "We tried as hard as we could, to save your daughter's life, but we were not able to do so. I am so sorry, but your daughter has passed away." Uttering those words caused a sickening and sinking feeling in my stomach and an anxious lump in my throat. Mom burst into tears, sobbing into her husband's shoulder. Dad just stared at me, in total disbelief. The younger siblings were slow to understand what just happened, not really comprehending and processing this terrible news. I silently put my hands on the knees of both the mom and dad, without speaking a word. After several minutes, I asked them if they had any questions for me. Some surviving family members have no further questions and want the physician to leave the room so they can grieve in private. Other families have many questions to which they want answers. This family had a lot of questions. With their prompting me for answers, but without utilizing gruesome detail, I explained her injuries and the extensive efforts we had made to prevent her death. I assured them that throughout it all, she was unconscious, unable to perceive pain, unaware of her surroundings, and that she did not suffer. After several more minutes, the pace at which the questions had come slackened until there were no more to be asked. I told them I was very sorry for their loss and left the room. It had to be apparent by my visage that I was genuinely and deeply saddened. This case hurt.

I went back to the physicians' room. It is a very small, closet-like space with a chair and coffee pot. I sat down. There were thirty-four other patients in the emergency department, all with an assortment of illness and injury, and I had to get back to caring for them. But first I needed to recover. I needed to regroup, gain my composure, and focus on my responsibilities. Over a period of two to three minutes, I gathered my thoughts, stood up, and pressed on. I started to care for the waiting patients. I had to force myself to concentrate on the tasks at hand.

Approximately twenty minutes later, the charge nurse approached and informed me that the family of the fallen teenager wanted to speak with me again. My mind raced. I became anxious. It was unusual for a family to ask to speak with me again after delivering such terrible news. What could they want to speak with me about? Were they upset at her care? Did I do something wrong? I gently knocked on the door and entered the room with trepidation. "I understand you requested to speak with me. Do you have some more questions?" The mom and dad were standing up, facing me but holding their hands and arms tightly around each other. "Yes," the dad stated. He was looking me straight in the eyes. Although his eyes were red from crying, his facial expression was silently communicating to me the importance of what he was about to tell me. It was a warm and engaging visual embrace. "We just want you to know that we recognize you did everything in your power to save our daughter's life. We want to thank you for being here, and for taking such great care of her. We understand that you did everything humanly possible. Her death is not a failure on your part. It is God who has called her to be with him."

This was the definition of guts. It was grace under pressure. At the most difficult, darkest hour of their lives, they took the time to reach out and thank me for taking care of their precious daughter. They were, in their own way, releasing me from any doubt or guilt I might harbor in failing to save their loved one. I immediately felt the heavy weight of responsibility for the inability to avert the death of their daughter taken off my shoulders.

This family, notably the mother and father, were truly special people. I wished so much that I had been able to save this child of theirs. As I now look back on this event, I have an overwhelming admiration for their steadfast belief in each other and in their Higher Power. They taught me, in retrospect, how powerful and liberating a true belief can be.

CHAPTER 10

A Nurse Saves a Life

A YOUNG, FEMALE, AND ACCOMPLISHED ATHLETE WAS training for a triathlon. She was swimming in a local lake with family members in a motorized boat trolling alongside assisting her training in a safe manner. Suddenly sensing something was terribly wrong with her body, she yelled to her family for help. Her father threw her a flotation device, but she did not reach for the device. Within seconds of her plea for help she had become unconscious in the water. The patient's sister frantically pulled her up and into the boat. The athlete was in cardiac arrest, meaning her heart was not beating, and she was not breathing. Family members took turns providing CPR, including her father and husband.

Using a cell phone, a 911 call was made from their speeding boat now racing against time back to the dock. Paramedics arrived via ambulance and used two advanced medical devices to try and save her young life. The first was a chest compression device (CPR) that provided mechanical and automated chest compressions. This automated chest compressor is more efficient and superior to manual chest compressions done by another person. The device encircles the patient's chest and has a plunger that is placed on the patient's sternum (breastbone). The plunger descends quickly downward, depressing the patient's chest two to three inches, then recoils upward, pulling the chest wall up with it. It provides consistent chest compressions and causes forward blood flow in the absence of a beating heart. The chest compression device was placed around her chest and began delivering its hopefully effective plunges to her thorax. The second device, an automated external cardiac defibrillator, was utilized to deliver a high voltage electrical shock to her heart. The electrical pads were placed onto her chest wall in the front and back and delivered 200 joules of electricity. Her body jerked upward with the release of electricity. Although the chest compression device requires medical training, the automated external cardiac defibrillator does not. These automated external defibrillators are designed so that a nonmedical lay person can safely and successfully use them. These automated defibrillators are now commonplace in public areas where large numbers of people are expected, such as sports stadiums and airports.

The combined therapies were successful on this athlete, and her heart started beating effectively on its own. She was transported expeditiously to the hospital, still unconscious, and placed on a ventilator in the intensive care unit. She had been without a heartbeat and ventilations for a significant period. The human brain can only tolerate a few short minutes of lack of oxygen and blood flow before irreversible neurologic injury occurs. This young athlete received high-quality CPR, but it is a guess as to its effectiveness in supplying adequate blood flow to the brain. The individual patient response to CPR, whether manual or automated, is highly variable, and depends on many factors, including individual patient's physical build and predisposition to disease, as well as the quality of the CPR being performed. As a result, although her heart was now in a stable rhythm and producing normal blood flow, her neurologic outcome was far from certain. Only time would tell if she would regain consciousness and if she would have a normally functioning brain.

Miraculously, she awoke the next day. Although unable to recall any of the entire event, she was neurologically normal, having suffered no complications from her cardiac arrest. Over the ensuing days, extensive cardiac testing was performed to determine the cause of her cardiac arrest. Why would a highly trained athlete in outstanding physical condition suddenly go into cardiac arrest? The diagnosis was eventually made. Prolonged QT Syndrome was the culprit. It is a condition that adversely effects the electrical system of the heart. Many times, it is a silent disorder that goes undetected until it causes a major arrhythmia and sudden death. An internal cardiac defibrillator was permanently implanted into her chest and heart as a precaution against future events. Should she experience additional life-threatening cardiac events, her life would not depend on being in the right place at the right time to receive efficient CPR.

An electrical shock by her internal cardiac defibrillator would alleviate the need for a nearby automated external cardiac defibrillator. She now carries her own personal internal cardiac defibrillator wherever she travels.

The inspiring part of this story is that this triathlete is an emergency room nurse. In fact, she is one of our emergency room nurses. One year before her own near-death experience, she had participated in a fundraising running race to benefit the local community. She finished first in her age category in that race. The funding she helped to raise was used to purchase the very chest compression device that was utilized by the emergency medical technicians to save her own life! Was this turn of events capricious and driven by nothing other than pure chance? Perhaps. I now view it as a thank-you. A just reward deliberately bestowed by a Higher Power to an individual who gave of herself. It also served as personal motivation—motivation provided by a Higher Power, to this young athlete—to continue her efforts in helping to save the lives of fellow human beings. I think it was a Higher Power communicating to her that her fundraising efforts are noteworthy and important. The encouragement from her Higher Power worked. Since her near-death event, she has greatly amplified her fundraising efforts for advanced cardiac resuscitation equipment that can be utilized by prehospital personnel to save lives. She has remained tireless and determined in this endeavor. Not only does she continue her humanitarian and altruistic work as a nurse, but she remains steadfast in raising significant amounts of monetary funds for the purchase of lifesaving medical equipment, as well as for training the lay public in CPR technique. She has greatly extended her circle of influence well beyond her local community.

CHAPTER 11

My Worst Shift Ever

I WAS WORKING AN 11:00 P.M. TO 7:00 a.m. night shift. It was summertime; the weather was uncomfortably hot and humid, and the emergency department was extremely busy. A basic tenet is the hotter the ambient outside temperature, the busier the emergency department. This night was no different. There was the usual summertime assortment of assaults, gunshot wounds, stab wounds, motor vehicle and motorcycle crashes, broken bones, and lacerations. I had a great team of nurses and resident-in-training physicians with whom to work. One of the nurses was a favorite of mine: hardworking, experienced, and reliable. If the place got out of control, I could count on her. The chief resident for the night shift, in his third year of emergency medicine training, was quite intelligent with a ton of common sense, which is a great combination of personal traits for an emergency physician to possess. He also was low-key and difficult to fluster, another bonus for what looked to be a very busy summertime night in the emergency department.

At the beginning of my shift, the incoming charge nurse informed me that there had been a "John Doe" earlier in the evening who had died from a cardiac arrest, and she was still trying to identify the patient in order to notify family. The "John Doe" patient had been rollerblading around the inner-city lakes district and was found lying unresponsive on the bike path with his rollerblades still on his feet. He was in cardiac arrest, had no signs of trauma, and had no identifying personal documents in his possession. He was pronounced dead after a failed resuscitation in the emergency department and was transported to the hospital morgue awaiting identification. I acknowledged this information from the charge nurse and set about the business of providing patient care.

At approximately 1:00 a.m., the nurse described above as one of my favorites came to me emotionally distraught. She informed me that she had received a telephone call from her sister. Her sister had developed a sudden and severe headache, and the nurse had told her sister to call 911 and have the ambulance come to our hospital. Approximately twenty minutes later, the ambulance transporting the nurse's sister arrived. I met this ambulance in the ambulance arrival ramp under the protective awning. Per verbal report, the paramedics had found the patient in severe painful distress, a little drowsy, but able to answer questions. During the ambulance transport to the emergency department, the patient had a markedly decreasing level of consciousness. I quickly assessed this patient while she was still laying on the ambulance stretcher in the back of the ambulance. She was unable to answer any questions and was barely responsive to painful stimuli. She was critically ill. I instructed the paramedics to take the patient directly to our critical care room, and I would meet them there. On my way to the critical care room, I veered off, found my nurse, the sister of this patient, and informed her that we would care for her sister in the critical care room, and that I would be out as soon as possible to give her an update.

The working diagnosis given the patient presentation was a subarachnoid hemorrhage. This is one type of stroke where there is bleeding into the subarachnoid space of the brain. It is usually caused by rupture of an aneurysm, a balloon-like outpouching of a brain artery. If the balloon-like outpouching gets thin enough, it bursts open, pouring blood into the subarachnoid space of the brain. This is a life-threatening emergency and can cause significant morbidity and mortality.

The patient was quickly administered intravenous medications to sedate and temporarily therapeutically paralyze her. A breathing tube was inserted into her trachea (throat), and she was placed on a ventilator. She was given an intravenous medication to control her blood pressure, which was severely elevated. Another medication was infused to prevent the blood vessels in her brain from developing spasm, which limits blood flow to brain cells resulting in more neurologic injury.

A rapidly performed head CT scan confirmed our suspicions and fears. A massive subarachnoid hemorrhage was evident. There was extensive bleeding. The likelihood of this patient surviving this event with a meaningful neurologic outcome given her clinical appearance and her CT scan findings was exceedingly small.

I sat down in a quiet room with my nurse, the sister of the critically ill patient. As gently as I could, I gave her the diagnosis and poor prognosis. I did my very best to console her, but overall, I felt helpless. I had done everything I could do medically for this patient. It was now up to the neurosurgeons and the patient herself to determine what would happen next and what would be the eventual outcome. The nurse left the emergency department and accompanied her sister to the surgical intensive care unit. I went back to work. There were forty patients in the department at the time. This was a busy shift, even by summertime standards.

Providing care to a critically ill patient who is a close relative of a coworker is stressful. There is self-imposed pressure in these cases. You want your management decisions to be perfect and your treatment to result in a great outcome. I knew that I had provided the correct care in a very timely fashion to this critically ill patient, but I was overcome with a feeling of futility. It did not seem like my interventions would make a difference. It was difficult listening to my other patients and render good medical care when my mind kept wandering back to my nurse's sister. What was happening to her now? I wondered if she would be a lucky one and beat the dismal odds. My training took over, and I began to focus on the patients at hand before me.

Over the next few days, this patient developed a myriad of complications related to her subarachnoid hemorrhage. Despite maximal neurosurgical support, her neurologic status continued to deteriorate, and she was eventually declared brain dead.

At approximately 3:00 a.m., on this, my worst shift ever, my third-year chief resident in training, who had helped me care for our nurse's sister, took a personal telephone call. It was his mother, who had called to tell him that his dad had gone out rollerblading around the city lakes during the early evening hours and had never returned home. She did not know where he was, or what had happened to him. Noticing that he was upset, I asked my third-year resident if there was something wrong, and if I could help. He told me what his mother had just told him. My third-year resident physician did not know there had been a "John Doe," a cardiac arrest victim that could not be resuscitated, earlier in the evening who was found wearing rollerblades on a city bicycle path. I do not want to ever again have the feeling I had the moment I realized the "John Doe" was my third-year resident's father. I experienced instantaneous, whole body, almost overwhelming anxiety, which I tried, probably unsuccessfully, to hide from this resident.

I guided the two of us to the quiet faculty room. We sat uncomfortably close on a sofa and I told him what I knew. The "John Doe" was obviously his father, now lying dead in our hospital morgue. But identification was still required in order to confirm the unthinkable. My third-year resident and I took an elevator down to the hospital basement and walked slowly in silence toward the locked doors of the morgue. I rang a buzzer on the wall, and within a minute the morgue attendant opened the heavy, cold, steel doors. I put my arm around the resident's shoulders as we entered the main room. The room was uncomfortably chilly, which exaggerated my already heightened state of anxiety. There were four dead bodies lying in this room, all covered with sheets. The morgue attendant silently pointed to the next to last table in the room. My heart raced as we slowly approached. We stopped at the table. I turned to the resident, asking him in a nonverbal fashion if he was ready, to which he responded with a minimal vertical nod of his head. I gently lifted the sheet off the patient's head and face, and my third-year resident burst into tears.

During the ensuing days, I was miserable and melancholic. I kept reliving the sorrowful events of my night shift. One thought repeatedly occurred to me. "Why did those terrible events have to happen on my shift?" It was a self-centered, egocentric, and selfish thought. I was feeling sorry for myself for having to endure the emotional pain of these two saddening events. Admittedly and regrettably, I gave cursory thought to my colleagues. Gradually I let the heartbreaking events of that night fade. Like many tragedies, emergency physicians store them deep in their memory, often sequestering those recollections to rid themselves of the painful experience and to have the ability to move on.

Weeks after this difficult night shift, after having returned to their jobs, both the nurse and the third-year resident approached me, independent of each other. Their words and thoughts were so very similar. They were incredibly grateful for how I ministered to them. They were indebted to me for how I managed what might have been their most painful night on this Earth. Now, looking back on those two conversations weeks after that fateful night, it finally dawned on me. I was there that horrible night for a reason. There was a purpose for my presence. I was there to care for and to console my colleagues. I was there to provide support, courage, and strength. My primary role that night was not as a physician caregiver. My role was to provide emotional support to coworkers experiencing terrible life events. I have come to comprehend that belief in a purpose in life necessitates a Higher Power. Without a Higher Power, there can be no faith or belief. When you have faith in a purpose for your life, you have faith in the presence of a Higher Power.

CHAPTER 12

One of Our Own

HE HAD RECENTLY GRADUATED FROM OUR EMERGENCY medicine residency training program. He had been a star scholar and athlete in high school and college. He excelled in medical school and was an outstanding resident physician. A life of serving others as a physician and of raising a family lay ahead for him. Unfortunately, his goals and dreams were never realized. While playing basketball with another recent physician graduate of our program, he developed severe chest pain. Shortly thereafter he suffered a cardiac arrest. His heart had stopped beating, and he ceased to breathe. He quickly lost consciousness. CPR was performed by his close physician friend for what seemed like hours but was measured in minutes. He underwent electrical defibrillation where metallic paddles were applied to his chest and delivered a powerful electrical shock to attempt to get his heart beating normally again. His body jolted and jumped an inch or two off the gurney. It worked. His heart developed a normal beat. He had a short "downtime," which is the time where his body and brain were without an effective blood pressure and adequate oxygen supply due to the cardiac arrest. As a result of that short downtime, and the excellent CPR he received, he awoke from unconsciousness just a few short minutes after receiving his lifesaving electrical shock.

This is where this tragic and sorrowful story becomes truly remarkable and extraordinary. This young, and talented physician, who had just been resuscitated from the dead, woke up, looked around the room, and then was…well…smiling. He had an infectious smile that would light up a room. It was a very distinctive, unique, and attractive smile. You could take a full facial picture with him smiling, then crop the image to just show his smile and you would still instantly know who it was! Upon awakening, he glanced around the emergency department examination room. These were surroundings with which he was intimately familiar as an emergency physician. He quickly surmised where he was and that something unusual must have happened to him. His gurney was surrounded by loving friends and family. "What happened to me? Why am I in the emergency department?" Despite not knowing exactly what had occurred, he continued to widely smile, which seemed odd to those surrounding his bed. He was quickly informed that he had suffered a cardiac arrest and had been brought back from the dead by CPR and a powerful electrical shock to his heart. He continued to exhibit what those surrounding his bed would describe as an inappropriate, wide-eyed smile given the circumstances. Smiling after being told your heart stopped beating and you needed four hundred joules of electricity to get it started again was conspicuously odd. It was incongruous. Perhaps he did have some brain damage! Why else would someone be smiling after just being told you almost died, and you still might die if your heart problem was not immediately fixed? After an awkward minute or two, his fellow physician friend just bluntly asked him with a hint of irritation in his voice "What the hell are you smiling about? You almost died!" The patient, our friend and colleague, went on to explain. He was not smiling because his life had been saved, although this would be deserving of a smile in and of itself. Rather, he was smiling from his near-death experience, which he passionately and ardently began to describe. He had been an avid trout fisherman from an early age. After his heart stopped beating and his brain stopped receiving adequate blood and oxygen, he stated he traveled "to the most incredible trout stream I have ever seen." In his words it was "stunningly beautiful, tranquil, and unbelievably peaceful." There was no trepidation. It was, as young people now say, "all good." His demeanor and facial countenance while he described his near-death experience conveyed an unmistakable emotional state—that of total serenity.

His visit to the trout stream was short-lived. He woke up to his vigilant friends and family while on an emergency department gurney. In the emergency department, continued low-grade chest pain and an abnormal electrocardiogram (EKG) were indications of an ongoing heart attack, and he was expeditiously transported to the cardiac catheterization lab where he was to undergo emergency cardiac catheterization. Make no mistake about it, he was happy to be alive and to find himself surrounded by those most important to him. As he described his experience, however, there were, at times, hints of regret that he had had to leave the trout stream. He had a glimpse of the afterlife, and the glimpse appeared to be a life-affirming as well as life-altering event. His demeanor was calm. He was very much at peace. He was not afraid of death. He welcomed the trip to the cardiac catheterization lab because he knew either way, no matter what happened or what the outcome would be, he would be at peace, and he would be in a good place.

Cardiac catheterization involves placing a large catheter (tube) into the femoral artery, floating a wire via the arterial system up into the coronary artery of the heart that was presumably blocked with a blood clot, which had caused his cardiac arrest. There, a balloon would be inflated across the blockage, and a short metal stent (tube) would be placed, opening the blocked coronary artery. This procedure has revolutionized the treatment of heart attacks. Although done routinely everyday throughout the United States, it is not without risk. Stroke, an abnormal heart electrical rhythm, and injury to the coronary arteries are but a few of the uncommon but real and possible complications. Unfortunately, he suffered another sudden cardiac arrest during the cardiac catheterization procedure, and again his heart stopped beating. The physicians and nurses in the cardiac catheterization room worked feverishly to save his life. They were not about to let a friend and a colleague heartbreakingly die at such an early age. Despite their heroic efforts, he could not be resuscitated. His heart simply refused to beat again. The physicians and nurses caring for their colleague, not to mention his family, were simply devastated. He died at the young age of thirty-two.

Word of his death quickly traveled to our emergency medicine residency training program. It was met with shock and disbelief and created a very empty sadness. He was universally well-liked. He was a beacon of hope. He was sunshine with a bright future. As hard as his death was taken, his near-death experience, subsequently re-layed to us, helped soften the blow. I have read a fair amount about near-death experiences, and there are several well-known books portraying such events. My physician-scientist mind reasoned in the past that near-death experiences were the result of a failing and dying brain. The lack of oxygen and blood supply would cause a dream like state, interpreted by the person who survives such an event as pleasant, comforting, and, in many cases, spiritual. Pleasant, near-death experiences could perhaps be some sort of protective physiologic mechanism the human brain has evolved to lessen the pain or agony of death. This was different. This was the first time I had heard it from a friend. Through my current retro-spective lens, I have come to believe that our friend did indeed have a preview of the afterlife. I am comforted in knowing that he visited that beautiful and tranquil trout stream for a second and an everlasting final time.

CHAPTER 13

Dignity Despite Disfigurement

HE PRESENTED TO THE EMERGENCY DEPARTMENT AT 4:00 a.m., in the middle of the night, when the department was likely to be less populated with patients and healthcare workers. The patient suffered from neurofibromatosis, and he was concerned he had an infection. Neurofibromatosis is a genetic disorder, which means you are born with the disease. It is characterized by tumors that slowly grow on nerve tissue. Since humans have nerves essentially everywhere in their body, these tumors can occur anywhere. The tumors are generally benign and noncancerous. People who have neurofibromatosis can have a wide range in expression of the disease and subsequent clinical appearance. The disease may be so mild as to be unnoticeable to the lay person, and in fact, may not even be recognized by an otherwise astute physician. It may cause only a few small bumps and/or a few flat, darker-pigmented lesions in the skin. On the other side of the spectrum, neurofibromatosis can be devastatingly disfiguring. It can cause large, fleshy, pedunculated tumors to grow all over the body, including the face. Individuals suffering from this extreme form might not otherwise be recognizable as humans, and they may look like something out of a horror movie. These deeply ill-fated people can develop hundreds, if not thousands, of these tumors.

My patient was such an unfortunate soul. This patient presented to me very early in my professional life. He remains the worst case of neurofibromatosis I have seen in my thirty-six-year career. His entire body was literally covered with these tumors. Some were small, but many others were large and hanging off his skin from thin stalks of tissue. Each tumor was positioned on top of another, leaving not one inch of normal, visible skin. This included his face. There was nothing remotely human about his visual appearance.

I have been accused of having a poker face, and not giving away my thoughts or emotions by changes in my countenance. For better or worse, it comes naturally to me. That night, my innate poker face skills were tested to the extreme. I tried to look directly into the eyes of this patient, but his eyes were virtually hidden in the mass of facial tumors. I tried to use my normal voice, my normal interaction, my normal questions, and my normal examination procedure. I did this so the patient did not suspect I was horrified by what I saw. I doubt I was successful in this regard.

I thought I understood why he came to the emergency department at 4:00 a.m. He did not want to scare anybody. He did not want to be gawked at. He had long ago been ostracized from society. I could not stop thinking how terrible this disease was for him, how lonely and desolate a life he must be living. How the only person who physically ever touches him must be a physician, like me. I touch him because it is my job. No one else would likely ever reach out and touch this man. Humans like to touch and to be touched by other humans. We like to handshake, pat each other on the back or shoulder, and hug. And of course, we like to have sexual contact. My best guess is that all forms of human touching for this man disappeared a long time ago.

If I had this disease, I have no doubt that self-loathing, self-pity, anger, and bitterness would be controlling and consuming my life. I doubt I would have survived to this man's age. Suicide would likely have intervened.

This man was a hermit. This was understandably so. But in my interaction with him, he demonstrated none of the emotions that would have dominated me had I had this disease. He was kind, soft-spoken, and introspective with an appropriate self-deprecating sense of humor. He seemed content, which is not what I would have anticipated. He was not bitter or angry, but rather he was amazingly grateful. He was grateful for the care I was rendering for his skin infection and open wound caused by one of his tumors. There was no mental misery or resentment. There was no melancholy. We talked about many things, albeit mostly superficial conversations about sports and weather. As I stated previously, this was early in my career as a physician. I did not have the people skills or the situational awareness to really note just how remarkable this man before me was. Had I been more mature as a physician and as a person, I would have spent a lot more time with him. It was 4:00 a.m., and the emergency department was not that busy. I would have broached the subject of living with his disease. I would have asked him his secret. How are you happy? How are you not bitter and angry?

At the end of my emergency department shift, I sat down with a medical textbook and read all about neuro-fibromatosis. I found that I learned new medical knowledge if I read about the pathology immediately after seeing a given case. It enabled me to put a so-called face to the disease. The face for this case was unforgettable. I read the cold hard scientific facts about neurofibromatosis. Just like a good doctor should. Years later, I now realize why this person came into my life, although ever so briefly. This man entered my life to teach me, and it was not to teach me about his disease. His lesson for me was not to be found in a medical textbook. We all have our crosses to bear, whether we have physical afflictions or difficult situations with unplanned adverse events in our lives. All of us have something heavy and unpleasant, if not just plain horrible, to lug around. Many of these crosses are foist upon us without having any control or say in the matter. These crosses can be obvious to all, like this man, or may be hidden and unknown to all, including loved ones. Some people, like this man, have bigger and heavier crosses to bear than others. Looking back, a Higher Power was present in this man. I truly believe this man was placed into my life (and I hope into the lives of others) to inspire, to mentor, and to provide an extreme example of the classic definition of dignity. Dignity can be described as self-respect, poise, pride, and self-worth. Yes, he avoided crowds and onlookers. But he avoided these social situations not because of shame or embarrassment, but because he truly did not want to frighten anybody, especially children. It took me many years later to realize how extraordinary this man was and how much I could have learned from him. Yes, he was afflicted with a terrible disease, but he was also given by his Higher Power an unbreakable spirit that was there for others to learn.

CHAPTER 14

A Five-Year-Old Boy
Teaches Forgiveness

THE CENTRALIZED ELECTRONIC LOCATOR BOARD IN THE emergency department indicated there was a five-year-old boy with an arm infection in room C8. When I entered the room, the patient was sitting on the examination bed along with his parents. I was immediately struck by this young patient's spontaneous smile. It was wide, genuine, and beguiling. His smile immediately put a smile on my face, a natural human reaction. It was, indeed, an infectious smile. I asked where he hurt, and he pointed to his right forearm. His parents were appropriately concerned, stating the process started four days ago as a simple pimple, but had progressively gotten worse. The parents questioned whether he could have been bitten by a spider. There had been no fever, chills, nausea, or vomiting, and his appetite had been good. There were no other medical conditions that could be contributory, such as diabetes. He had never had a problem like this before.

I lowered myself by bending at the knees and crouching to the floor so that it appeared he was bigger or taller than me, a way to try and put him at ease. This friendly maneuver was not necessary. He was already at ease, which was unusual. Most five-year-old patients in the emergency department with a painful condition would be undoubtedly concerned about the possibility of painful procedures. Needles were always the number-one concern for children this age. They are old enough to remember their last vaccination. I asked if I could look at it closer, and he raised his forearm toward me without hesitation and without any suspicion or fear that I would hurt him with my examination. He was either totally trusting or just naïve to the pain that doctors can inflict during an examination. It was a large abscess (i.e., a boil). It was close to two inches in diameter, and was raised, red, and just plain angry looking. I did not have to touch it to know if it was fluctuant. Fluctuance is the squishy feeling of fluid under the skin, a sign the lesion was full of pus. There was no doubt it was an infected abscess. Treatment with antibiotics would simply not suffice. The boil needed to be incised and drained. That meant taking a scalpel and cutting into the localized infected pocket, thereby releasing and draining the pus. An additional part of the incision and drainage procedure is making sure there are no smaller walled off or hidden pockets of pus within the lesion. Not only must I make an incision, but the procedure calls for placing a small hemostat, a kind of a scissors without sharp edges, into the open wound, and blindly exploring, probing and breaking open any smaller pockets of pus protected by adhesions and scars. If it is not done correctly, the abscess would not be adequately drained and would not resolve. Draining an abscess is a painful procedure. Smaller abscesses can be drained using only local anesthesia. Larger abscesses, and especially those with adhesions and smaller pockets of pus within the large abscess, are very difficult to anesthetize locally. As a result, it is common to administer medications by intravenous or other means to help reduce the pain of this procedure. You can administer varying levels of medication, from enough to just take the edge off the pain, all the way to complete, deep sedation and amnesia.

My assessment was that draining this child's abscess would be a very painful procedure. Just the extensive infiltration of local anesthetic in and around the abscess would be painful, let alone breaking up the adhesions. I recommended to the parents that we start an intravenous line and give medication through the IV to have their child be sedated. It was a much more humane approach. Unfortunately, the parents would not consent. During my disclosure of the potential risks of sedation, I appropriately indicated the most serious complication would be respiratory failure, which is stopping breathing. I was careful to indicate that we would have all the needed personnel and equipment in the room should that happen, and we would breathe for their son until he started breathing on his own again. I explained that we sedate many patients every single day in our emergency department, and it is a very safe procedure. The parents were frightened. No matter how I tried to assuage their fear, they could not get past the stop breathing part of the informed consent process. I told them if this was my son, I would sedate him for this very painful procedure. Still no change in their stance. After what seems like many minutes and several different approaches to changing their mind, it was apparent I would be performing this under local anesthesia. The parents did consent to some oral pain medication before the procedure was performed, but I knew this would not suffice.

The child was a trouper. He handled the extensive local anesthetic infiltration with the needle by silently shedding some tears, but there were no screams, and more importantly to me, he kept his arm still during the anesthetic infiltration so as not to cause injury to himself or to me by suddenly moving or withdrawing his arm. I was impressed by the self-control this five-year-old had over his fears. I was pleasantly surprised by how well he managed his emotions, and I hoped this would portend favorably to the actual incision and drainage procedure itself. I allowed enough time, not only for the local anesthetic to take maximal effect, but to give this child some time to regroup, dry his tears, and get mentally prepared for the next part. The incision was easy as the skin was well anesthetized and produced no pain. However, the abscess pocket was complex, and would need the probing and lysis of adhesions that I had been worried about. After warning both parents and this child about my next steps, I proceeded to use a hemostat and break up the smaller pockets of pus I encountered. Unfortunately, this caused pain. Significant pain. I tried to be quick and efficient, talking my way through the procedure to try and divert attention, and to minimize the amount of time the pain would need to be endured. He cried throughout the short procedure, and screamed once. But he never moved or flinched. It was over in literally twenty to thirty seconds, but the procedural pain would need some time to rescind. I loosely packed his abscess hole with gauze, dressed his wound, looked him straight in the eye and told him how impressed I was with his bravery. I attempted to give him a high five with his good arm, but his enthusiasm was lacking, and he meekly raised his good arm toward mine, mostly because his parents were encouraging him to do so. Frankly, I did not blame him for his lukewarm high five. I felt like I had betrayed his confidence and trust in me. I told his parents he would need to return to the emergency department in two days to have the gauze packing removed and the abscess site reassessed.

This child came back in two days with his parents, and I happened by chance to be on duty when they arrived in the emergency department. As I was walking toward his examination room, I fully expected to find this patient to be timid, reserved, clinging to his parents, and exhibiting caution if not outright fear of my presence. After all, I had inflicted significant pain on this child just two days previously. It would not have surprised me if the child would not allow me to take off his dressing and examine his incision and drainage surgical wound. I was totally wrong. When I opened the examination room curtain, the child, who had been sitting on the examination bed, immediately jumped up and off the bed, and gave me this ear-to-ear, full-toothed smile! He swiftly bounded to me just a few steps away, and gave my legs a tight, several-second hug! Amazing. I had tortured this child just two days ago. Yet his instinct was to hug me and give me thanks. He was not mad at how I had caused him pain and not at all concerned that I might be causing him some more pain in a few minutes when I removed the gauze packing from the deep wound. It was just a recognition of my helping him and his expression of gratefulness. That reaction is innate. It cannot be taught. It cannot be contemplated, planned, or contrived. It was as natural a reaction of gratefulness as I have ever witnessed. This was a gift from a Higher Power. But it was not a gift to me from a Higher Power, but a gift from a Higher Power to this child. A gift of being able to see beyond the pain. A gift of being able to give onto others. A gift of being able to forgive. Forgiveness sets the forgiver free, and gratefulness is a gift unto itself. This is what I learned from this five-year-old child.

CHAPTER 15

Suicide and a Second Chance

SHE PRESENTED TO THE EMERGENCY DEPARTMENT IN a coma, the etiology of which was completely unknown. She was accompanied by her two sisters, who were visibly and rightfully distraught. They had no idea as to why they found their sister at home in a deep state of unconsciousness. They had gone to her house to pick her up for a movie and found her in her current state laying on the kitchen floor. There was no medical history to account for her altered mental status. Immediately sensing something was terribly wrong with their sister, they called 911.

The very first thing I noticed as I walked into the examining room was her abnormal breathing pattern. She was kussmaul breathing. This is an abnormal respiratory pattern in which the patient's breaths are as deep and as fast as the human body allows. Many conditions can generate kussmaul breathing, including severe infection, exposure to a toxic substance, and diabetic ketoacidosis. Diabetic ketoacidosis is the most common cause for kussmaul breathing, at least in my anecdotal personal experience. Diabetic ketoacidosis occurs in poorly controlled diabetes, when a patient's blood sugar increases to dangerous levels, causing the patient's blood to become more acidic. The pH of our blood is normally 7.4. Our bodies have millions of chemical interactions that depend on the human pH being stable and exactly at 7.4. The body will try to correct for an abnormal blood pH in a myriad of ways so that these millions of chemical interactions can continue to successfully occur. Acidosis is a blood pH less than 7.4. Kussmaul breathing is one of the mechanisms the body uses to correct for an abnormally low (acidotic) blood pH. Any condition that causes severe acidosis can lead to kussmaul breathing, which is the body's way of adapting and autocorrecting the acidosis.

After introducing myself to her two sisters, who were seated at the patient's bedside, my first question was a general one. "What happened?" It was readily apparent they had no idea as to what was wrong with their sister. My second question to the sisters was based on the patient's kussmaul breathing. "Was your sister on any medications, particularly for sugar diabetes?" I thought this was a good starting point in obtaining the diagnosis. But the patient was not diabetic and had a normal blood glucose level measured by the paramedics who brought her to the hospital. My third question came out of nowhere. To this day I am not sure why it was my third question, as there were dozens of other more important and obvious questions to ask, such as the presence of recent head

trauma, recent complaint of headaches, medication history, or alcohol and illicit substance abuse. It must have
been unconscious pattern recognition on my part. "Has
your sister been depressed?" The answer from the sisters
was affirmative. She had been quietly suffering from
depression, but to the best of their knowledge she had
not sought psychiatric help and was not on any medications for depression. Her depression seemed to be deepening over the past couple of months, and taking her
out to a movie was indeed a deliberate ploy by her sisters
to help elevate her mood, if only temporarily. However,
there was no suicide note, no empty pill bottles, and
no physical evidence of a self-inflicted toxic ingestion.
Nonetheless, I was overcome with a strong intuition of
what had occurred despite a complete lack of objective
data. I found myself suddenly stating "I think your sister
has tried to kill herself, and my guess is that she drank
car antifreeze."

This was a big leap of faith on my part. I had nothing to substantiate this bold assertion, and I was going
to look silly if I was wrong. The patient's sisters looked
at me with an odd combination of flattering awe at my
intuition and a sincere distrust. How in the world do you
come to that diagnosis without anything but a couple of
questions? I had not even performed a physical examination, let alone diagnostic medical imaging and laboratory testing, on their sister yet. I followed my intuition,
and within a few minutes after emergency lab testing, the
diagnosis was confirmed. Their sister had ingested a toxic dose of ethylene glycol, which is readily found in car

antifreeze. Only small amounts of swallowed ethylene glycol are needed to cause death. It causes severe acidosis in the blood and would account for her kussmaul respirations. It can rapidly cause severe kidney, cardiac, and brain injury. Time was of the essence. It was clinically apparent that she had ingested enough to result in death.

The patient was moved into our critical care room. I inserted a breathing tube into her throat and placed her on a ventilator with deep sedation. I administered specific intravenous antidotes for ethylene glycol poisoning. I inserted a very large intravenous catheter into her jugular neck vein and arranged for emergency hemodialysis that would remove any of the remaining ethylene glycol toxin in her blood. She was admitted to the intensive care unit. She had a very long, and difficult hospital course. She barely averted death on several occasions. Her case could be defined as a great case from an emergency physician's point of view. Great cases can be defined as infrequently seen and very complex cases that pose a diagnostic and therapeutic challenge to the physician. It should be noted that great cases are not necessarily great from the patient's perspective. I followed her care in the hospital on a very peripheral and distant basis. I just wanted to know her outcome. Did she live or die?

Sadly, that is all I wondered about this patient at that time. I say sadly because that is, indeed, all that mattered to me. Had I done my job well enough to save this woman's life? It was the ultimate emergency physician ego boost. I did not think for one minute what had led this patient to try and claim her life, nor did I contemplate how she was doing after failing her suicide attempt. Maybe she was mad at me for foiling a well-thought-out suicide plan. I suspected she was still depressed postattempt, and my personal bias, based on prior patients, was that her chances of long-term happiness were dismal. I had seen many depressed patients attempt suicide on more than one occasion. It would not surprise me if this patient continued to be depressed and attempted suicide in the future. But that was not my problem.

As it turns out, she lived. She completely recovered without any neurologic, kidney, cardiac, or pulmonary consequences. She quickly became a distant memory for me, getting lost among the thousands of patient interactions I had before and after our two lives crossed paths. I forgot all about her.

But she had not forgotten about me. Her near-death experience was a life-changing event for her. In the months after her nearly successful suicide attempt, she battled back from the depths of depression and put her life back together. This was not an easy task, and it was not without significant challenges. She stumbled at times but climbed relentlessly. She eventually decided to volunteer at my hospital, where her life was saved. Five years after her almost successful assault on her own life, she decided she wanted to meet me. She had contemplated reaching out to me often after her physical recovery. Up to this point, five years after the event, our time together was limited to the hour or so she spent in the emergency department, during which time she was totally unconscious.

She tracked me down by way of an intrahospital letter. She wanted to meet the physician whom her sisters credited with saving her life. My taking credit for saving her life would be disingenuous. Hundreds of hospital workers were involved in saving her life. I just got the ball rolling on the correct path. We met together with a friend of hers that she brought along for emotional support. We gave each other an immediate hug, unusual for strangers meeting for the first time. This hug was indicative of the emotional element felt by both of us at this meeting. Meeting her was one of the highlights of my professional career. She had written and published a book about her near-death experience from a nearly successful suicidal ingestion. In writing the book, she hoped to inspire others that depression can be conquered and teach others that happiness is a skill that can be acquired. I read her book with intense interest. It was a riveting account of her journey down into and up out of depression. In her book, in plain sight and in an unapologetic fashion, is her belief in a Higher Power. It was this belief that was the foundation of her recovery. It enabled her to make the long, slow, difficult climb out of depression and attain happiness. She is now without depression and is medication-free.

In looking back, her battle and victory over depression and suicide is inspiring. She is now giving her time and energy to the hospital that saved her life. She wrote and published a book telling her personal and painful story with the sole purpose of helping others not to attempt suicide or to help those who have attempted suicide to recover. She, like her Higher Power, provides hope to those who despair. She is a living testimony that faith and courage, through a belief in yourself and in your Higher Power, can overcome desolation and despondency.

CHAPTER 16

A Life and Death Handshake

We had a one-minute warning. An ambulance, traveling with lights flashing and sirens blasting, was about to deliver to the emergency department a young male who had suffered a gunshot wound to the chest. There had been no direct communication from the paramedics as to the patient's condition. This usually meant the paramedics were too busy treating a critically ill or injured patient to talk with us over the emergency radio system. We started massive preparations in getting medical equipment and medications readied for immediate utilization. On arrival to the emergency department, the patient was comatose, with slow, agonal respirations indicative of a critically injured patient. The paramedics were augmenting his inadequate respirations by applying a plastic mask to his face and compressing an attached bag full of oxygen. He had a single round wound in a very bad location, directly over his heart in the front of his chest.

We immediately inserted a breathing tube into his throat and placed him on a ventilator. His pulse was measured at 160 beats per minute on the cardiac monitor, and it was weak and difficult to palpate.

This type of case can best be described as organized chaos, because there are many different diagnostic and therapeutic maneuvers being done simultaneously by six to eight nurses and physicians at the bedside. A quick cardiac ultrasound examination was performed by one of the emergency physicians. Most lay people are familiar with the use of ultrasound in pregnancy. In traumatic injuries, it can quickly inform the physician of life-threatening injuries and their locations. In this case, it revealed that the fibrous sac (pericardium) that surrounds and encases the heart was filled with blood and was deleteriously squeezing the heart. This compression prevented the heart chambers from effectively filling with blood. As a result, his heart was having extreme difficulty in pumping blood out to the rest of his body. Although the heart was beating fast and strong, it was not filling with blood, and an insufficient amount of blood was being pumped outward to the rest of his body and brain. The blood in the pericardial sac most assuredly came from the bullet damaging some part of the heart, causing leaking of blood from the heart into the pericardial sac. Before we could even think about what to do next, his heart rate slowed to thirty beats per minute, and his pulse could not be palpated.

A quick look with the ultrasound showed a heart with extremely weak and slow contractions. This was a sure harbinger of imminent death. He had been in the emergency department for one minute at this juncture. There was no time to take this patient to the operating room. He would be dead before he arrived in the operating room. Per protocol, a left thoracotomy was performed. This operation involves making a large incision into his left chest. After the incision is made and the left chest is opened, rib spreaders are placed to gain full access to the heart and left lung. The sac that surrounds the heart was filled with blood and was extremely tense. Our suspicion based on the cardiac ultrasound was correct. He had suffered a cardiac wound and had bled into the pericardial sac. This essentially choked his heart and caused his heart to stop beating. The pericardial sac was opened. An impressive amount of blood spilled out of his left chest onto the gurney, as well as onto my cover protected shoes. A quick inspection revealed he had a single wound to his heart. The bullet had hit his right ventricle from an acute angle, making a dime size hole as the source of bleeding. His heart started to beat wildly and strongly within thirty seconds of relieving the choking pressure that had been caused by the blood-filled pericardial sac.

My finger plugged the hole in the now strongly beating heart, and I was able to slow down the hemorrhage. Arrangements were quickly made to take him to the operating room for formal exploration and repair of his cardiac wound. His pulse became faster and stronger every second. My plan was to place a couple of metallic cardiac staples to temporarily close the cardiac wound until formal operative cardiac wound closure was performed in the operating room. His blood pressure normalized.

Now the unanticipated happened. My left index finger was plugging the hole in his heart. I had the cardiac stapling gun in my right hand. Without warning, the patient lifted his right hand and arm, reached across his own chest, and grabbed my left hand as it entered his left chest cavity! That was the hand that was keeping him from bleeding to death. *What in the world...?!* I was stunned. But it quickly made sense. He presented in a coma, with a barely beating heart and virtually no respiration. He clinically died immediately upon arrival to the ED. The chest incision was performed when there was no pulse, and no blood was being pumped to his brain. He was basically dead at that point in time. His brain had stopped working, and he had no ability to sense or feel pain. The normally intensely painful procedures of inserting a breathing tube and cutting an incision into his chest cavity were performed without sensation or awareness. There had been no time, and indeed no need, to give this patient anesthesia. However, his heart started beating so quickly and effectively after relieving the pressure of the blood-filled pericardial sac, that his brain function came roaring back to life. He was quickly given intravenous anesthesia, and he became unresponsive to all physical stimuli.

At the time of the incident, I viewed this simply as appropriate physiologic responses. He woke up with my hand inside his left chest, plugging a hole in his heart. Of course he was going to reach for the unpleasant physical stimulus and pull it out. Although totally unexpected, it was, nonetheless, a reasonable physiologic response. This is one of those cases you do not forget. It was easy for me to recall the specific details of this case. Now, in retrospect, did this rare interaction offer something more that I had missed? Indeed, it did. The message was hidden in HOW this patient reached for my hand. He did not reach for my hand as most patients did who were having an unpleasant stimulus. Most patients reach, grab, and then either push or pull the stimulus away, attempting to remove the stimulus. I have given unpleasant, noxious stimuli to thousands of patients to assess their level of consciousness as part of their physical examination. It is a diagnostic maneuver utilized to assess how well the patient's brain is working. This noxious stimulus would normally be in the form of a vigorous sternal rub. Sternal rub means using your knuckles and pressing and/or rubbing hard on their sternum (chest bone). Patients who had a high enough level of consciousness to react to this would invariably reach for my hand, grab it, and lift it off their chest wall, or push my hand away, thus stopping the noxious stimulus. This is a normal response that should occur in a patient whose brain is functioning relatively well.

That is not how this patient with the penetrating cardiac injury reacted. Rather, he slowly reached across his chest, grabbed my hand, and squeezed. He did not try to pull or push my hand away. He just took it and firmly squeezed. I reflected on the nature of that hand squeeze. It was as though he was shaking my hand. It was a friendly embrace. It felt like an acknowledgment that he knew he was critically ill, and he knew, despite the pain, that we were trying to save his life. It was as though he was trying to communicate with me. I remember putting the cardiac stapling gun down that had been in my right hand and squeezing his right hand as it squeezed my left hand, thereby acknowledging his handshake. His handshake was a thank-you. It was an acknowledgment that he knew someone was trying to save his life. He was telling me he was alive, and he wanted to stay that way. My right hand grabbing a hold of his right hand was simply my rejoinder.

This patient went on to a complete recovery. A few days after his operation, I visited with him in his hospital room, hoping to further share that moment of attachment we had in the emergency department stabilization room. I was simultaneously disappointed and relieved to learn that the medications and anesthesia administered to him in the emergency department immediately after his brain came back to life had provided retrograde amnesia. He recalled absolutely nothing of his sixteen minutes in the emergency department. Awakening during an operation is a fear for both patients and physicians, and I was glad to learn he did not recall anything. But

I was also disappointed. It was a special moment I will never forget, and I wanted to share it with him again.

CHAPTER 17

A Miracle

WE RECEIVED NO ADVANCED WARNING FROM THE ambulance, who had just brought us a nineteen-year-old male patient who had sustained a diving injury. This patient, along with several of his friends, went to a local lake in order to escape the summer heat. He dove off a dock into a lake, not cognizant that the lake was very shallow at this location. His head hit the sandy bottom, and he immediately sustained a severe cervical spine (neck) injury. His friends, fortunately, quickly recognized his paralysis and inability to move. They immediately waded into the lake and pulled him to safety. The patient was awake and breathing with some forceful effort. 911 was called from a cell phone. The paramedics arrived at the scene and appropriately placed him on a protective backboard and transported him to the hospital, keeping his neck immobilized and without any movement.

His neurologic examination was upsetting to all the healthcare providers in the emergency department stabilization room. He was unable to move his hands, arms, legs or feet. He was having difficulty breathing because his chest muscles and diaphragm were not working well. His ability to feel a pinprick was absent below his collar bone. He had priapism which is an abnormal penile erection. Priapism in this setting is an involuntary reflex that has no sexual connotation, but rather is indicative of a severe spinal cord injury. His rectal examination revealed the total absence of rectal tone, meaning he had lost the ability to self-control his bowel movements or his urination. Everyone in the room, including the wide-awake patient, knew he had suffered a devastating injury. There was little conversation. I leaned over the patient, enabling me to speak in a whisper to create the illusion of a private conversation despite the presence of many other healthcare providers in the vicinity. I explained what I thought was wrong. He did not need me to educate him. He seemed to know full well the tragedy unfolding in his life. He knew his life was about to be completely transformed, from one of unlimited possibilities to one of severe and permanent physical restrictions. Normally the trauma room is full of talk. Physician orders, examination findings, and lab results are verbalized to all the healthcare personnel present. It was strangely, almost sickeningly, quiet. After my brief conversation, it was evident the patient understood everything. From then on, he had no interest in further conversation. He asked no additional questions. The only motor activity this patient had demonstrated was a flicker of movement in the toes of one foot, and it was transient and not reproducible on command. His physical examination was ominous.

This constellation of signs and symptoms indicated a complete spinal cord injury, where the spinal cord was either transected, or crushed and severely damaged. The prognosis in such an injury is horrible. Patients never have any meaningful recovery from this type of injury. He would be confined to a bed and could be ventilator dependent for the rest of his life. He would never voluntarily move again. The patient, completely awake, could sense his fate. To bear witness to a teenager, completely healthy thirty minutes ago, transformed into a living nightmare was heart breaking.

We set about our work. We cared for this patient as best we knew how. A neck x-ray confirmed our fears. He had a severe fracture/dislocation between his fourth and fifth neck vertebra. The spinal canal, the space where the spinal cord resides, is normally at least twelve millimeters wide at the level of his injury. The x-ray demonstrated his canal width was reduced to a few millimeters due to the dislocated and abnormal position of the vertebra. The radiographic appearance mandated the spinal cord to have suffered a devastating and irreversible injury.

The patient was lightly sedated, and Gardner-Wells tongs were placed into his skull bones. This is a device used for reduction of fractures and dislocations of the neck vertebra. It has a metallic ring that is attached to the skull by pointed screws that are bolted into the skull. The ring is then attached to a rope with a pulley system, and gradual weights are added to the pulley system, placing the neck vertebra in longitudinal traction. Multiple x-rays are then taken each time additional weight is placed, with the goal of normalizing the alignment of the neck vertebra. This procedure would restore spinal canal width. This was accomplished readily in this patient, and within ninety minutes of his head hitting the bottom of the lake, the normal alignment of his neck vertebra had been restored. This would not, of course, result in regaining any motor or sensory function. The damage to the spinal cord occurred at the instant of injury and normalizing the alignment would not result in any improvement. The damage was done, and there was no going back. At least that is what medical science as known at this time would indicate.

What started to occur next stunned every healthcare worker in that room. Approximately twenty minutes after normalizing his neck anatomy, he slowly began to regain function. It started in his toes, and slowly, gradually, seemingly inexorably, marched upward. He left the emergency department for the intensive care unit starting to bend his knees. His arm and hands remained flaccid. We had no idea just how much return of function he would eventually regain. By the textbook, he was not supposed to be moving anything ever again. Any optimism was guarded at best, if not just plain unrealistic.

Yet his recovery continued in the intensive care unit. Within hours he was moving his thighs, hips, hands, and elbows. The short story is that he regained all his motor and sensory function. It looked as though his spinal cord was never damaged. He had an operation to stabilize his neck bones and was discharged from the hospital seven days later completely neurologically intact without any motor or sensory deficits.

At the time, I was shocked by the outcome. My colleagues and I published a scientific paper detailing this case because such recoveries are not supposed to happen in patients with complete spinal cord injuries. In reviewing the medical literature and thinking extensively about this case at the time, I came to believe that the spinal cord had not been transected, only badly pinched, resulting in spinal cord shock without actual nerve cellular injury. That is the logical conclusion arrived at by my medical training at the time of this case.

Thirty-three years later I am writing this book. This case, indelibly etched into my mind, now takes on a different meaning. If you called this a miracle, I would not argue with you.

Here is another take on the events of this case. The trauma room, usually noisy and bustling, was eerily quiet during the care of this young patient. Healthcare workers were doing their job, but in silence. I never asked any of the dozen or so healthcare workers who were in the room that day what they were thinking while silently going about their business. Yet I have come to believe that all of us were praying. Whether it was formal pleading to their Higher Power or just simply wishing and hoping this patient well, all of us were beseeching in some manner. For me, at that time in my life, I did not pray to a Higher Power. I did not think there was one. But I remember having an intense feeling of wishing this person well, of wanting him to have the strength of character to come through this and emerge on the other side with hope. I now recognize that this intense feeling I experienced was indeed a thinly veiled form of prayer.

I fully believe there was a collective prayer event that unfolded in the silence of this case. This has all the earmarks of a miracle. If you do not call this a miracle, I am not sure you will ever call anything a miracle. Our silent communal prayers were answered.

CHAPTER 18

A Spontaneous and Selfless Act

THE EMERGENCY MEDICINE RESIDENT PHYSICIAN IN TRAINING was exiting the emergency room at 8:00 a.m. after a long and difficult night shift. He was halfway through his third and final year of emergency medicine residency. He was six months away from achieving an educational goal that he started pursuing almost twelve years earlier. The relentless pace of physician training in the specialty of emergency medicine was starting to wear him down. The last night was a typical night shift. He had probably cared for thirty-five to forty patients during his twelve-hour stint. There had been several patients with gunshot wounds from the same street incident, a bad motor vehicle crash with multiple patients that were critically injured, and an overdosed patient who arrived awake and talking, only to suffer a cardiac arrest and die shortly after emergency department arrival, despite all attempts at resuscitation. There had been no shortage of critically ill patients requiring acute decision-making and emergent invasive procedures. Tired, he had nothing else on his mind except walking to his nearby apartment as quickly as he could and crashing asleep in his warm bed. The start of his next demanding twelve-hour shift was only eleven hours away. His apartment was a mere ten-minute walk away. However, it was January, and the ambient temperature was well below zero that morning, notwithstanding a brutal wind-chill effect. He remembered hearing something on the news about a polar vortex, and how it was going to be dangerously cold for the next several days.

He stopped at the double glass doors of the emergency department entrance. He buttoned his overcoat, lowered his wool cap over his ears, and adjusted his scarf to cover his entire face except his eyes. He shuddered at the thought of his cold walk ahead. He took a small step forward toward the doors, and that is when, out of the corner of his eye, he noted one of our "regulars." This patient was well known to the emergency department staff and visited us on many a night. He was homeless and had suffered a traumatic leg amputation several years ago. He preferred using a wheelchair to either crutches or a prosthetic limb. This wheelchair partiality existed because he drank large quantities of alcohol daily. The wheelchair provided more stability when intoxicated than either crutches or a prosthetic limb. He would present to the emergency department intoxicated and was usually extremely belligerent and combative. You had to be careful with him, as he was known to take roundhouse fist swings at healthcare workers. It was not a lot of fun to care for this patient when he was acutely intoxicated.

It seemed that he divided his time between a homeless shelter and the emergency department. There was sort of a routine in caring for this patient. He would arrive in the evening to the emergency department intoxicated, often with a blood alcohol level three or four times over the legal limit. He would be undressed and examined to make sure he did not have any new occult injuries that his level of intoxication might have otherwise hidden or suppressed. His clothes, frequently soiled with urine, would be washed and dried. He would be carefully observed over the nighttime hours, and then once awake and coherent in the morning, given his now clean and dry garments and released back into the world. He would eventually wheel his way back to the nearby shelter, and at some point, start the cycle all over with another bottle of booze.

This night had been no different. The third-year emergency medicine resident physician had assigned himself to care for this patient ten hours before. Initially agitated, verbally abusive, and physically aggressive toward this third-year resident physician, the patient eventually passed out and slept the alcohol off. The emergency medicine resident physician performed a quick physical examination, noted no new injuries, and set the plan in action to release him in the morning. It was now morning, and the patient had been discharged from the emergency department.

This regular was also readying himself for his cold wheel back to the local shelter, which was several blocks away from the hospital. The regular was buttoning his coat and pulling his hat low over his ears. But the third-year resident physician, ever the astute clinician and on the lookout for problems, noted this regular did not have any winter gloves. There was no way for this regular to wheel himself in a wheelchair without his hands contacting the cold rubber and metal of the wheelchair. It was cold enough outside to cause severe frostbite to his exposed fingers in just a few minutes.

There was no hesitation. There was no fanfare. The third-year resident physician took off his own warm and expensive winter gloves, walked over to the regular, and simply gave him his winter gloves, quietly whispering "I think you need these more than I do." Without waiting for an answer from the regular, the third-year resident physician walked out the double glass doors with his hands tucked into his winter jacket pockets. He gave his expensive and warm gloves to the very individual who just a few hours before had taken a wild swing at him in his drunken and agitated state.

The third-year resident physician never mentioned this selfless act of giving to anyone. Had it not been surreptitiously witnessed by a triage nurse, it would have gone unnoticed and unknown. When I prepare myself to go out into cold winter weather by putting on my warm, winter gloves, I often think of this exchange. I consider that there must be an almost infinite number of similar acts of kindness in our world daily. Most of these selfless acts go unobserved. I like to think that the number of kind acts performed daily on this Earth exceeds by trillionfold the many terrible atrocities that seem to always get widely reported in the news. It is the almost infinite number of daily altruistic and self-sacrificing acts by humans the world over that are a reason to have faith.

CHAPTER 19

A Mother's Love for Her Child

We received a radio call from an incoming ambulance. The paramedics were five minutes away from the hospital with a seven-month-old infant who was in respiratory distress. The infant had been crawling on the floor of his home when he suddenly developed severe respiratory distress. The infant had been well with no signs of illness earlier in the day.

The ambulance arrived at the emergency department, and rather than keeping the infant on the ambulance gurney and rolling the patient in, the paramedic elected to simply scoop up the infant in his arms and run the short distance from the ambulance port down the hallway to the emergency department critical care room. It was the fastest way to deliver the infant to us. The team of nurses and physicians who were going to care for this small infant stood in anticipation, surrounding the empty critical care bed. Watching the large double doors to the stabilization room burst open with a paramedic literally running to place this infant onto the bed in front of us was surreal. It was summer, and sweat was pouring off the brow of the paramedic. There was no mistaking the meaning of the paramedic's actions, facial countenance, demeanor, and brow sweat. This infant was in trouble.

The infant's face was cyanotic, a medical term for a deathly blue color. It is usually from ineffective breathing. The infant had agonal respirations, best described as gasping, superficial, labored, irregular, and not compatible with life. It is a respiratory pattern frequently seen immediately before all respiratory effort stops. This infant would cease breathing altogether at any second. We quickly attempted to bag-valve-mask ventilate the patient. This entails using a plastic mask that is attached to a bag into which high-content oxygen is delivered. The mask is placed over the infant's mouth and nose, and the attached bag containing the high concentration of oxygen is squeezed, forcing oxygen into his lungs. Within a few short compressions of the bag, it was apparent the infant had a significant problem. Our attempts at bag-valve-mask ventilation revealed extremely high airway pressures. The bag resisted the physicians squeeze. As hard or forcefully as we would squeeze the bag, the air would not go into the infant's lungs. Instead it leaked out the small crevices between the plastic mask and the patient's facial skin. Attempting to obtain a better seal between mask and facial skin only resulted in increased difficulty of squeezing the bag. There was no chest rise normally seen with inspiration and squeezing the ventilation bag.

There really is only one thing that could make a totally healthy, normal infant without any traumatic mechanism suddenly unable to breath. The infant had a foreign body somewhere in his airway which was blocking the passage of air. The blockage was high grade, meaning no air was getting to his lungs, not even with forceful bag-valve-mask ventilation. The foreign body could literally be anything that was small enough to get into the airway, but large enough to obstruct. The location of the foreign body could be anywhere as well: from the back of his mouth, to resting on his vocal cords, to inside his trachea (windpipe). The nature of the object and its location would determine the success or failure in this life-threatening emergency. One thing was certain. This infant was choking to death. Within a minute of emergency department arrival, the infant's agonal respirations ceased altogether, and the infant became limp. There was no pulse. CPR was started. We prepared to insert an endotracheal (breathing) tube into his trachea and place him on a ventilator. Looking down into his throat, no foreign bodies could be visualized either in the back of his throat or sitting atop his vocal cords. This meant the foreign body was deep into his trachea and impossible to see and remove in a timely manner. If we could not establish a patent airway in this infant within the next four to six minutes, severe brain damage and likely death would result. The tube went into his trachea readily, but when attempting to ventilate directly via the tube, high airway pressures were again encountered, just like the failed bag-valve-mask ventilation. The therapeutic options now were extremely limited. The infant was without a pulse or respiratory effort, and we were unable to breathe for him. Within a few short minutes, his brain would be dead from lack of oxygen.

We decided to forcefully push the tube in his trachea as far in as it would go. The hope was that we could push the foreign body down his entire trachea, and into one of his lungs. This would then open the other lung, and we could ventilate one lung, thereby providing enough oxygen delivery. Several attempts to do this occurred, but to no avail. The foreign body remained in the trachea and could not be pushed downward. A last-ditch effort was performed. We placed a needle into the front of his neck, into his trachea, and attached the needle to high-pressure oxygen powered tubing. This would provide high-pressure oxygen delivery, hoping to forcefully blow the foreign body down his trachea and into one lung. Again, this proved futile. The infant, after thirty minutes of heroic attempts to save his life, was declared dead.

This was an extremely difficult case, from the moment the paramedic burst into the room carrying this infant to my declaring him dead. Total silence gripped the room for several minutes. No one spoke or even moved. We just stared either at the infant lying motionless on the bed or at the floor. You could literally hear the proverbial pin drop. After several minutes, I gathered the medical students, interns, and residents in training into a small circle within the critical care room. It was time for me to teach. Looking back, this was one of my coping mechanisms. I had a job to do (i.e., save the infant), and when that did not happen, I took up my second responsibility, which was teaching the resident physicians in training. The nurses went about their business of cleaning up the infant so the family could view their precious loved one.

After my quick three-minute lecture on the management of foreign body airway obstruction, my attention turned to the family. I was told the mother was in the waiting room, and she was completely unaware of what just transpired. She did not speak English. I briefly met with the interpreter and explained what had just happened, and we walked into the family room together.

As I entered the room, the mother glanced at my face, and she immediately sensed from my visage that something bad had happened. No words were exchanged. The interpreter was superfluous. This mother instinctively knew I was the bearer of the worst news a mother could hear. She was completely alone, with no other friend or family support present. I gave this stranger a hug. I may have crossed some cultural barriers in doing so, but it seemed like the right thing to do. After what felt like an eternity, I spoke about what had happened. At least what I thought had happened. An autopsy would need to confirm our working diagnosis. The mother wanted to see her little baby, and I walked her into the emergency department critical care room. She picked up the baby who was wrapped in a small blanket, cuddled and held him tight, like she probably had done hundreds of times in the past seven months since his birth. She wept, as did many of the healthcare workers witnessing this mother-infant interaction in the room.

At the time, I was heartbroken. This tragedy fit the motif of previous catastrophic events I have witnessed as a physician. Events that were unfair, cruel, and seemingly arbitrary. I could not explain why stuff like this happens. It made me both mad and sad. I was not sure how to direct my anger. At the time of this event, I did not think about religion or God.

Why am I telling and reliving this tragedy? As I recalled this event, I began to see another side of this calamity. What I began to see is the innate and genetic instinct mothers have for their children. Teleological thinking (i.e., the explanation of phenomena by the purpose they serve rather than by postulated causes) makes the relationship a mother has with a seven-month-old infant somewhat perplexing. Impartial observation from a distance would reveal this infant to have been a tremendous physical and mental burden for its mother. This infant would cry every time he wanted to be fed or have his diapers changed or be made warmer or colder or to just be held. This infant deprived his mother of sleep, rest, and personal time. This infant completely uprooted this mother's life, and by necessity became the center of her attention. Infants really are self-centered little human beings. This mother's life over the seven months of this infant's existence had been fully occupied by demands from this little human. This infant had never said "Thank you" to his mother, or "I love you, Mom." The most this mother likely had received back from this infant was a smile.

Yet despite the relatively short time this infant had been in the mother's life and the total and complete control this infant had over the mother with his incessant demands, a mother's love was absolute and unconditional.

Here was a mother weeping over the loss of her infant. A mother's love is so profound and so deep that all the inconveniences of motherhood simply pale in comparison. This mother's love goes back to the beginning of humans. It is instinctual and intuitive. It is powerful to observe. I have witnessed a mother's love much earlier than in a seven-month-old infant. Indeed, I have seen it expressed when mothers see their infant in utero via ultrasound. I have seen it in mothers grieving after a miscarriage. It is overpowering and inspiring.

A toy balloon, found at the autopsy which I attended, was tightly wedged at the end of the trachea, and was straddling into both the left and right lung. The nature and location of this foreign body precluded successful resuscitation. The infant never had a chance to be saved. His death was a fait accompli. Which is also how one could describe a mother's love for her child.

CHAPTER 20

Laughter:
The Best Medicine

WORKING IN THE EMERGENCY DEPARTMENT OF AN urban, level 1 trauma center for thirty-six years, I have witnessed all aspects of the human condition. It can be an emotional rollercoaster, with uplifting highs as well as lows down to the depths of despair. Sometimes, though, it has just been plain fun. I will tell you about two cases that whenever I recall them, still bring a smile to my face. In both cases, please realize that, at the time of the event, we were not laughing at the patient, but we were laughing along with the patient!

A young man was changing a flat tire on his SUV motor vehicle. At some point, while handling the new, large, inflated tire, he managed to stick his index finger through one of the lugholes. It was a tight squeeze, and for some reason he pushed his finger all the way into the lughole so the finger base, where the finger joins the hand, was abutting the wheel hub. To his surprise and concern, he was unable to remove his finger from the lughole. All home remedy efforts, such as soap and lubricant, failed to free his index finger. His finger began to swell, the sharp edges of the lug hole were starting to cut into his finger, and he realized he was going to need some professional help. He decided that professional help should be an emergency physician!

He called two of his buddies to help him carry the firmly affixed tire, as his arms started to grow weary from lifting the heavy object, and he certainly could not drive in his condition. So, into the emergency department strode the three of them. The patient was in the middle with the pinned index finger and his two friends on each side supporting the large tire.

At first, a lot of head scratching occurred. How in the world are we going to get this off? This was before the advent of high-speed hand-held rotary cutting tools. Those devices have simplified the removal of human anatomic parts that are entrapped in various objects. Virtually all the healthcare providers in the emergency department were enlisted and queried for their ideas. Soon enough, the hospital's building and maintenance crew were summoned for their ideas as well as the mechanical tools at their disposal.

As you can imagine, the air was filled with humor. The humor started with the patient himself. Self-deprecating humor is a distinctly human trait. I don't think it exists elsewhere in the animal kingdom. It was this patient's self-deprecating humor which emanated throughout the emergency department and fostered, well, kind of a party atmosphere! The jokes kept coming, along with many harebrained and half-baked ideas to free the finger. Perhaps the best and easiest suggestion came from the patient himself. "Let's just cut the finger off, save us all some time and effort, and go find a bar!"

The method of removal of this trapped finger from the tire lug hole that was decided upon required many sets of hands. First, a nerve block with an anesthetic was performed at the level of the patient's wrist to alleviate pain that would be encountered during the finger extrication. The tire was elevated to the level of the patient's head, and the finger protruding out of the lughole was tightly wrapped in dental floss, starting at the fingertip, to force the finger swelling and edema to recede. Then, four or five three-foot-long, thin strips of gauze were soaked in petroleum jelly and forced through the lughole between the finger and the sharp edges inside of the lughole, so none of the finger was touching the sharp edges. The three-foot-long strips of lubricated gauze were pulled tightly on each of their ends. Finally, the tire was rotated back and forth, repeatedly and ever so gently, until after several minutes the large first knuckle slipped through the lughole, freeing the finger. No lacerations. No broken finger bones.

A loud cheer permeated the emergency department!

The second memorable case filled with humor was an elderly man who presented at 3:00 a.m. to the emergency department. He had caught a very large snapping turtle in a local lake earlier in the day. He had killed the turtle by decapitation and was planning on using the turtle for food. He had placed the decapitated turtle head into a waste bucket. At some point, he reached into the bucket, and accidentally placed his left thumb into the open mouth of the turtle's head. The turtle head reflexively chomped down hard on his thumb! Try as he might, he could not loosen the turtle's firm hold. As with the patient with his finger stuck in a tire lughole, this patient decided he also needed the professional services of an emergency physician. Into the emergency department walked this patient with a very large, decapitated turtle head firmly attached to his left thumb. Having this patient appear with this problem was certainly a way to make the early morning hours pass more quickly. It was also a welcomed diversion from the usual human calamities that tend to show up in the emergency department at those hours.

This patient turned out to be extremely entertaining. He was humorous and self-deprecating. He also was a walking Wikipedia article on snapping turtles. He knew everything about snapping turtles, from life and reproductive cycles, to their preferred diet and their natural enemies. He had no education beyond high school, but he clearly was intelligent, inquisitive, and obviously enthralled with snapping turtles. He did not just hunt, kill, and eat them. He appreciated and admired them as an integral part of nature. I learned a lot about snapping turtles that night. Do you want to know the most memorable tidbit of information I learned that night? Decapitated turtle heads will continue to reflexively bite down when something is placed in their mouth for up to nine days after decapitation! What a fact to know!

We obtained two pairs of pliers from our buildings and grounds maintenance department, locked onto the upper and lower jaws of the turtle, and pried open the mouth of the turtle, thus freeing the finger. The patient was extremely grateful. The turtle head maintained an open mouth position, and when looking at the turtle head from directly in front, the turtle appeared to be smiling. Or maybe that was just what my tired, three o'clock-in-the-early-morning mind conjured up.

"Truth is stranger than fiction, but it is because Fiction is obliged to stick to possibilities; Truth isn't." This quote is attributed to Mark Twain—I think a fitting quote for both patient encounters in this narrative.

If you just look around at the human condition, there are all sorts of funny, "Are you kidding me?" story lines. The ability to laugh at ourselves is part of what makes us human. Laughter does more than release stress and make us feel good as individuals. When humans enjoy a common laugh, appropriately and assuming it is not at the expense of another human being, it serves as a connecting mechanism. It serves to bring us closer together and helps us endure the low points in life and withstand the painful events in our lives. Self-deprecating humor improves psychological well-being. It marks us as unique. It makes me think that my Higher Power has a funny bone.

CHAPTER 21

Why Do Bad Things Happen to Good People?

ANSWERING THIS QUESTION REMAINS A CONSTANT CHALLENGE for me. I could write an additional two hundred pages in this book with stories of patients who got a raw deal in life. Patients who, by no fault of their own, had to live an existence that most people looking in from the outside world would describe as totally miserable. This is especially true when confronted with pediatric patients. I have seen firsthand many pediatric patients suffering from circumstances with which they have no control. Examples include the four-year-old female patient who was sexually assaulted by a relative, the two-year-old boy who required amputations of both hands and feet after suffering an infection which attacked his limbs, the five-year-old who developed leukemia and suffered a brain hemorrhage, causing permanent and severe cognitive deficits, and a three-month-old infant, accidentally smothered to death when sleeping in a bed with his mother.

The seemingly daily onslaught of human tragedy displayed in emergency departments is not limited to pediatric patients. Examples of adults abound. A fifty-year-old father of two diagnosed with Amyotrophic Lateral Sclerosis (ALS or Lou Gehrig's disease) who has a precipitous downhill course of the disease and becomes bedridden and ventilator dependent. A thirty-five-year-old female diagnosed with Huntington's disease, destined for progressive and severe mental status changes and a harsh physical and neurologic disability. A previously healthy seventy-three-year-old physician who dedicated his entire life to the care of those in need announces his retirement. He is about to enjoy his golden years with his family, only to be diagnosed with pancreatic cancer and pass away a few short months after his retirement.

It gets even more personal for me. My mother, a person who was generous, kind, and self-sacrificing, not just to her family but seemingly to everyone, who was religious to a point of piety, was diagnosed with Alzheimer's disease at the young age of sixty-seven. I watched in horror as this disease slowly and relentlessly stole her personality and essence, reducing her to a shell of the incredible person she had been. What is the "purpose" of this disease? Why does this disease and others exist?

Is life just a weird and, at times, cruel game of chance? A game of unpredictable roulette? And why or how does a Higher Power play this game? Do we live in a universe where the Higher Power is hands off, exhibits no control, and lets whatever is going to happen, happen? Why? If our Higher Power is a laissez-faire administrator to this universe, it seems like he (she) is underachieving with an awful waste of ultimate supreme power.

I cannot answer these questions. Not with any certainty. Nor can any human. It is not within our purview to know. After my spiritual awakening and out of necessity, I adopted both a professional and personal approach when confronted with human tragedy that seems to help me cope and gives me the strength to continue in my job on the front lines of human misfortune and sorrow.

When challenged with heartbreak, I simply tell myself that this patient, this horrible event, came into my life for a reason. The reason may be that I am, for whatever reason, uniquely in a position to help. Maybe that's a little too self-centered or egotistical for some readers. I do not look at it that way. They came into my life at this moment in time for a purpose. Not because I'm better, but because I have a purpose. I try to answer that purpose as best I can. I don't always feel like I get it right. I do not always feel like I make a difference. A physician's first and foremost responsibility is to cure; to take away the pain; to change a patient's life circumstances for the better. Using that as a criterion for making a difference, it is no wonder I often feel like I have failed. The bar is way too high. There is a myriad of things in life that we simply cannot fix, or for that matter, even make better. And so, the feeling of personal failure. However, occasionally I am reminded that I don't have to cure an illness, or take away the physical pain, or heal an injury to make a difference in a patient's life. In fact, I can answer the purpose that comes with my interaction with a patient in need without even knowing it.

One interaction that I had with a victim of rape stands as an example of helping without cognizance. It is an example of fulfilling my purpose with a patient without any understanding or even knowledge of that purpose. At the time I did not feel I had accomplished anything. I only remember this interaction because of what happened a day later. Had it not been for what transpired the next day, I would have long ago forgotten about this patient, as I have taken care of hundreds of sexual assault victims over the years. The interaction was straightforward and similar to hundreds of my prior interactions with victims of rape.

I walked into an exam room with an emergency department nurse to care for a young woman who was eight weeks pregnant and had been sexually assaulted by an ex-boyfriend. I took an abbreviated history from the patient, and performed a physical examination minus the pelvic examination. I performed a quick bedside abdominal ultrasound examination to document the presence of a viable intrauterine pregnancy with cardiac activity. As there were no physical injuries, I left the room and called for a sexual assault resource nurse to perform her pelvic examination. This sexual assault resource nurse would collect evidence samples and carefully document in the chart her clinical examination findings so that detailed data would be available for any criminal charges that might be filed in the future. I spent roughly eight to ten minutes with this patient. I went on to see my next patient, and this victim of sexual assault was destined to be a foggy memory, like those before her.

However, the next day, I found in my hospital mailbox a handwritten note from the emergency department nurse who helped me care for this patient. Here is the note, verbatim:

"We saw a patient together yesterday in B5. She talked at length with me about how you made her feel. She said you had a spirit that made her feel safe and cared for. She really appreciated when you came in to tell her you called in a special nurse…another message that you cared for her. She said from your eyes she could tell you cared and your calm voice and gentle touch made her feel calm and safe. She showed me how gently you touch her abdomen. She looked over at you while you were doing her ultrasound and she felt you had no idea the impact you had on her. I thought you should know what a profound impact you had on this patient and the strength that gave her to go forward and work things out in her life. I admire you for having this incredible bedside manner in light of all that you see and do in our emergency department."

I was truly humbled by this compliment. The truth is that I did feel like I had done anything special. I do not recall feeling particularly empathic or sympathetic during this encounter. The emergency department at the time was awash with all sorts of patients needing care, and I did not have the time nor energy to deliberately show compassion to this patient. I needed to be efficient, do my job, and move onto the next patient in need. Obviously, I did something positive to have had such an effect on her. The point is that this patient came to me for a reason. There was purpose in our meeting. We both had a purpose. My purpose was to soothe her mental anguish, to make her feel safe and cared for. I did not see, feel, or recognize my purpose at the time of our meeting. I would have remained ignorant of that purpose save for the note the nurse provided the following day. But I firmly believe that my purpose was fulfilled in that meeting, even if unknowingly fulfilled. I could not erase her memory of the rape or take away her pain and mental suffering. She did not have any physical injuries for me to help mend. But I was able to make her feel safe and cared for, even for a temporary moment in time. Likewise, she had a purpose in our meeting. She was there to help me to become a better physician and a better human being. I think she accomplished that, even if I did not recognize it at the time.

CHAPTER 22

Humans Helping Humans

OUR CRITICAL CARE ROOM IS CALLED THE stabilization room ("stab room" for short). It is relatively large, holding up to four critically ill or injured patients at once. Each of the four separate areas of the room has all the equipment to resuscitate a patient from anything that may befall them. Any condition in which there is a good chance of loss of life, limb, or severe morbidity merits care in this stabilization room. The stab room is a room where seconds count and life hangs in the balance. It is not a room for the faint of heart. Visually gruesome traumatic injuries from a seemingly unlimited number of mechanisms are common. Gunshot wounds, knife wounds, severe injury from motor vehicle crashes and falls from significant heights, extensive burns, and physical assaults are a daily and common occurrence. Medical conditions such as heart attack, stroke, severe allergic reactions, respiratory distress from pneumonia or asthma, overdoses, and drownings are frequently encountered. The stab room is all-inclusive, from the newborn to the centenarian, both sexes and all sexual orientations, all skin pigmentations and genetic facial countenances, all socioeconomic levels, and all religious and political beliefs. Despite the wide variety, and this is crucial: all patients are treated equally.

It is not unusual for patients to present gasping for what might be their last breaths of air without immediate medical intervention. Many times, these traumatic and medical conditions are enveloped and veiled in a thick emotional cloud. Severe trauma from child abuse is an example. It can be gut-wrenching to provide care to these little ones. I have cared for many "shaken-baby" infants and child victims of deliberate blunt force trauma. I have an odd and conflicting mix of emotions during these cases. Sadness, furious anger, empathy, compassion, confusion, and doubt swirl in my head. I strive to heal one human, while wanting to punish another human. A second example is the patient who deliberately ingests a lethal dose of a substance, be it a prescription medication, over-the-counter medication or illicit drug. This patient presents awake, talking, and in no significant distress. This patient is subdued and regretful of their impulsive suicidal action, but once the toxin starts to have its affect, it renders the patient critically ill, followed by inevitable death, despite heroic efforts to save their life. Over 6,500 patients per year, or eighteen patients per day, are wheeled or carried into the stab room. Each has their own story to tell. Each patient is unique.

The stab room is manned with staff physicians, nurses, nursing assistants, respiratory therapists, pharmacologists, resident physicians in training, and medical students. Additional human resources come to the bedside depending on the type of case and the needs of the patient. There is a minimum of eight healthcare workers for each case, and more become involved as needed. Some of the more complicated cases will see the number of healthcare workers assigned to that case swell to fifteen or more. Each healthcare worker has their predetermined role and tasks.

Some of my most memorable moments as an emergency medicine physician took place in the stab room. As I retrospectively and introspectively examined my stab room experiences in writing this book, a most powerful thought occurred to me. No matter what role any of the ten or more healthcare workers were playing in caring for any given patient case, there was a common, underlying thread. We were all there for the same purpose: to help another human being. This overwhelming sense of collective and communal compassion starts before the patient arrives by ambulance to the stab room. When notified of an incoming ambulance carrying a patient with a gunshot wound to the chest, the stab room is set in motion. Various packs of sterile instruments are opened, the ventilator readied, and syringes are prefilled with powerful medications. It is ten or more healthcare workers bonding through a common purpose. After roles are assigned, and the room completely physically readied, we stand, wait, and mentally prepare. Often, we wait in silence. It is at this precise moment that I note how kind, altruistic, loving, caring, and self-sacrificing a species *Homo sapiens* is. Yes, it is our job. And yes, we are getting paid to do this job. But it is a job with sacrifice. Healthcare workers have exposure to blood-borne pathogens, exposure to physical harm by agitated and combative patients, exposure to the emotionally charged and draining scenarios that can lead to posttraumatic stress disorder, and exposure to the consequences of therapeutic failure and the loss of a life. Extremely infrequently, we make mistakes, costing the patient and their family pain and suffering that could or should have been prevented. We, as healthcare workers, must come to terms with our fallibility. These are some of the real-life dangers posed to healthcare workers in these stab room cases. Yet in the heat of the battle, in the middle of a case where blood seems to be everywhere, where there appears to be a somewhat controlled chaos, humans help humans. We help humans who are not our friends or family. They are strangers to us. I don't believe for one second there is anything other than motivating altruism in the heart of every healthcare worker who is working under these difficult conditions in the stab room. It is remarkable to see and even more remarkable to feel. I have been privileged and lucky to have been able to participate.

I have ridden all too often the emotional rollercoaster that occurs in the stab room. From the elevating highs associated with saving someone's life, to the debilitating lows concomitant with a patient dying unexpectedly. In cases of unpredicted patient death, there is the inevitable second guessing. Should I have done something different, or sooner? Would that have made the difference? Each case culminated in a walk to the family room, where members of a patient's family and circle of friends would await your presence. This is perhaps more stressful than the actual event itself. As a thinking, self-aware species, we all know that death, in the long run, is unavoidable. We just never expect it to happen *today.* Telling family and friends that, for their loved one, today is the day, is perhaps the most difficult thing a human can do. We, the healthcare workers who cared for a deceased patient, can mitigate the overwhelming sense of loss experienced by the family and friends of the patient by conveying through our words and actions that we care, we understand, and we tried our best to help.

CHAPTER 23

The Empty Critical Care Room

Most of the time when I am in the stabilization room, there are one or more critically ill or injured patients present with a multitude of healthcare givers focused on saving life and limb. But I have, from time to time, entered the stabilization room alone, without any of the noise and hustle and bustle of critical care. Pardon the medical black humor, but at these times when I am in the room alone, it is deathly quiet. It is a well-insulated and protected room, keeping out the noise of the surrounding ED, and more importantly, keeping the sounds of critical care, which can at times be horrific, within its four walls.

When I enter alone, I walk silently around the room. There is medical equipment everywhere. Each glance at a specific device brings memory flashbacks of cases from the past—sad and disheartening cases as well as enlightening and uplifting cases. It is amazing how the human mind works. The isolated visual cue of a piece of medical equipment instantly brings on the sights, sounds, and smells from long ago cases, as well as the immediate development of the associated emotions and feelings related to that well-remembered case.

As I stand in silence, the same thought seems to creep into my mind. Who is the next human being who will be lying on the complex and very expensive operating table gurney in the stab room? What will their clinical problem be? What will be the age of the patient? Will it be trauma, medical, pediatric, obstetric? Will it be a life-changing or life-ending event? Will they be conscious and aware, or unconscious, with their fate in the hands of the healthcare-providing strangers in the room? Will it be a clinical problem I have seen dozens, if not hundreds of times before, or something totally unique, rare, and thus incredibly challenging and difficult to manage?

It is a safe bet that the next patient lying on that operative table gurney in the emergency department stabilization room did not expect to be there that day. Neither did their family. We humans rarely think about the all-too-possible bad things that might be in store for us. No one awakens in the morning thinking, "I might have a bad car crash today, and be in the emergency department with a punctured lung, ruptured spleen, and a pelvic fracture," even though every day, people end up in our stab room with those injuries after such an occurrence. Events happen each day that change life circumstances on a dime, and some of these events end those lives.

A confession that I have not told anyone, so now I guess I am telling everyone: Sometimes during these solitary excursions through the stab room, I lay supine on the operating table gurney and imagine myself to be the patient. I look up at the stark ceiling, at all the medical equipment looking down on me and surrounding me. I imagine looking up at the faces of healthcare-providing strangers, who are staring down at me, contemplating what to do with me. I look at the digital clock on the wall. And I wonder when my time will come. When will my life be changed forever, or ended in an unexpected flash? How will that unfold? When will I be laying here, totally dependent on the strangers surrounding me? If I am awake, will I be brave and stoic, or frightened and panicked? Will I be accepting, docile, or fighting to the end? I have seen the entire gamut of human emotion in this setting. How will I react? Will I be ready? I can honestly say that since a nondescript little metallic pipe slipped over an ordinary metal flange after sardonically asking a question for my then nonexistent Higher Power, I am more ready than I have ever been.

Likewise, I am a better physician. Not in terms of knowledge or skills, but in terms of human interactions. By laying on that operating table in the quiet and empty stab room, I am much more aware of what my patients are feeling, thinking, and experiencing.

CHAPTER 24

The Landlord

AN EIGHTY-TWO-YEAR-OLD FEMALE PATIENT PRESENTED FOR EVAL-
UATION of injuries suffered in a fall. The circumstances of
this case are all too familiar to an emergency physician.
This frail patient had fallen in her apartment kitchen
and had suffered a broken hip. She did not wear a medical alert device and had no cell phone on her person at
the time of the fall. Unable to walk or even crawl, she laid
on the hard kitchen floor for eighteen hours until being
discovered and rescued from her predicament. 911 was
called, and an ambulance promptly arrived, transporting her directly to the emergency department.

In the emergency department, the patient was awake
and conversing, but in obvious physical pain. She was
also in significant mental anguish and emotional pain.
The physical pain was easy to explain and readily evident. Her right leg was shorter than her left and rotated
at an unusual angle. Broken hips are quite painful. In addition to her broken hip, she had developed open pressure sores from laying on the hard floor for a prolonged
amount of time. Her lips and tongue were bone dry, and

her skin elasticity was poor, all indicating moderate dehydration. She had not had anything to eat or drink for over a day.

Emergency physicians see many patients a day, most of whom are in some sort of painful distress. Our response to patients in pain is tempered by an almost constant exposure to patients in pain. It is not that we don't care about a patient's pain. Alleviating pain is a very rewarding experience and one of the most important responsibilities we have as physicians. However, it is important to appropriately match our perceived degree of pain to the correct management of the actual pain being endorsed by the patient. Morphine is not appropriate for pain associated with a minor laceration, and acetaminophen is not appropriate for management of severe burns. This patient was clearly in significant pain, and I would be able to alleviate that pain to a large degree. In this patient, however, it was her mental and emotional state that really bothered me much more that her physical pain. She appeared severely emotionally traumatized by the ordeal. Not the trauma related to her broken hip, but the trauma to her psyche. The more I put myself in her shoes, the more I realized just how awful an event this was for her. She lay, on the floor, unable to move, with severe pain. No food or water was available. She was alone, and no one seemed to be aware of her plight. No one noticed her absence, nor did anyone seem to care. She was frightened and panicked. It must have occurred to her that she may be laying on her final resting spot. Dying is frightening. Dying alone is terrifying.

But she was not going to die, nor was she totally alone. Her landlord made sure of that. Her landlord had noted that this patient had not picked up her morning news-paper in the common mailroom area of the apartment complex. This patient was a creature of habit, and she al-ways picked up her mail and daily newspaper at virtually the same time every single day. When he discovered that this patient had not picked up her mail in her usual time frame, he went to her apartment, entered, and found her on the floor. The total emotional reprieve and release upon seeing her landlord must have been enormous for this elderly woman.

This landlord made it a habit of checking in on his el-derly, at-risk, tenants. Not by knocking on doors or mak-ing phone calls. Doing so would seem to the landlord as invading his tenant's privacy. Rather he checked in on them in more subtle, but just as effective ways. Stopping by the common mailroom daily and making sure his at-risk elderly tenants were picking up their mail in a timely fashion consistent with their usual routine was one such inconspicuous method of observation. This landlord did not have to do this. This was not a senior high rise. It was not in his job description as a landlord to watch over his flock of vulnerable older adults. No one would ever fault him for not deliberately looking after his tenants. Nonetheless, he did.

The landlord had followed the ambulance to the emergency department in his own car. The patient had no family to speak of, and the landlord was aware of this. The very fact the landlord knew this patient had no family was testimony to his caring nature. He stayed by her side throughout the prolonged emergency department visit and accompanied the patient up to her hospital room. Once in her room, she would be prepped for surgery. It was a Saturday. I am sure the landlord had many other things planned for his day that did not include spending eight hours in an emergency room and hospital. Nonetheless, he did with nary a complaint.

Before the patient left the emergency department and was admitted to the hospital, I took the opportunity to thank this landlord. I told him that he may very well have saved this patient's life by his selfless actions. Despite my truthful praise, he was nonchalant, unassuming, and completely humble. In fact, he was almost embarrassed. His speech and mannerisms conveyed that this episode was not about him and his actions, but about the health and well-being of one of his tenants. I asked him about his building and his other tenants. During our conversation it became apparent to me that this landlord was a special person. In a nonbravado style, he told me of the various other ways he keeps tabs on his at-risk tenants. For example, he is on the lookout for the normal trash take-out and grocery delivery habits of his renters. It was apparent he did this not to make sure his tenants were treating his property well or for any other self-serving reason. This was total altruism at its finest. I asked him, bluntly, why he does this. His answer was so simple and yet so elegant. "It seems like the right thing to do." Wow. Are you kidding me? If all human beings used these words as their guiding philosophy in how to relate and interact with other human beings, ours would be a much better world in which to live.

I came away from this encounter not with the sadness of an eighty-two-year-old patient with a tragic and potentially life-threatening event. Rather I came away invigorated, hopeful, positive, and encouraged. There are many "landlords" out there, doing self-sacrificing deeds of service for their fellow human beings—a reason to have faith.

CHAPTER 25

A 90 Percent Burn

WHEN A PATIENT SUSTAINS A SEVERE BURN covering greater than 90 percent of his body, it is thought to be a universally fatal injury. There are virtually no survivors of such an injury. I had the pleasure and honor to work with one.

A young man presented to our hospital after an accident left him with second- and third-degree body surface burns covering 90 percent of his skin. He spent close to a year in the hospital undergoing an untold number of operative procedures and skin grafts, and he survived many near-death complications. When all was said and done, this remarkable survivor walked out of the hospital. You would think that most people who spent that amount of time in a hospital undergoing many painful procedures would have developed an aversion to hospitals and the medical profession, avoiding them at all costs. Such was not the case with this gentleman.

This year-long medical event changed the direction of his life forever. It changed what he wanted to do with his life and how he wanted to spend his time. He decided he wanted to give back. He wanted to thank the dozens if not hundreds of people who had worked diligently to save his life. He wanted to help other patients. It was not in the cards for him to attend medical or nursing school, so he gave back in the best way he could and in the way that was available to him: he worked in the emergency department, the same emergency department where he came for the initial resuscitation and treatment of his severe burn injury. Our emergency department. He worked as a unit clerk. His job entailed answering the emergency department phones, gathering the necessary paperwork for those patients being admitted to the hospital, working with the hospital bed placement office securing inpatient rooms, facilitating intra- and interinstitutional conversations between doctors, and relaying information between incoming ambulances transporting critically ill or injured patients and the receiving emergency physicians. It is a hard job. It is not at all glorified or glamorous. The emergency department is a very busy and active place. At any one solitary moment, there are a million events occurring in the emergency department. Virtually all of these events are important in delivering high-quality medical care. Many of these are time-dependent tasks that fall under the responsibility of the unit clerk.

He came to work with a smile on his face, and the smile stayed on his face throughout his entire shift. He was a hard worker, and he never complained. He never talked about his hospital or burn experiences. It was never about him. It was always about giving back. I admired him. He was given lemons, and he made lemonade. He converted a dreadful, painful, and surgery-filled, tragic year into a motive for him to alter the course of his life into a truly meaningful and altruistic epoch. He was the best kind of leader. He quietly led by example.

CHAPTER 26

The Universal Language

HE WAS A SEVENTY-NINE-YEAR-OLD MALE WHO HAD immigrated to the United States three days ago from Ethiopia. He came to the emergency department because he could not urinate and was having significant abdominal pain from bladder distension. He spoke Amharic and not a word of English. Given his age and diagnosis of urinary retention, the most likely cause was prostatic hypertrophy. This is where the male prostate gland becomes larger with increasing age and can result in the inability to urinate. Bladder distension is quite painful, and the treatment is to drain the urine by some method.

We spoke through a female interpreter. Despite the ability to communicate through the interpreter, who expertly converted English to Amharic and then back to English, I could not help but feel a wide and deep divide between patient and doctor. We spoke different languages, came from hometowns a half a world away, possessed markedly different cultural beliefs, came from different religious backgrounds, and were separated in age by many years. Despite my attempts at establishing a good, though temporary, physician-patient relationship to help guide us through this visit, I did not feel successful in doing so. I explained what I thought the reason was for his inability to urinate and the initial treatment. The initial treatment, of course, was placement of a bladder catheter (plastic tube) through his penis and into the bladder to drain the urine. I was uneasy. Here I was, listening to the young, female, American born interpreter explaining the necessary invasion of genitalia that belonged to a seventy-nine-year-old male patient who was in his third day in the United States. His countenance could be summed up in one word: stoic. There was no hint of emotion, and I had no idea how he was receiving and reacting to this information.

When I specifically asked if I had his permission to place the bladder catheter, he showed little emotion. He simply nodded his head up and down. It has been my anecdotal experience as a physician that when a male patient of any age agrees to have a plastic tube inserted into his penis and guided up into his bladder, he must be experiencing significant pain. Why else would a male allow that procedure to be performed, other than to alleviate intolerable pain? Despite his stoic and calm appearance, he was suffering. The bladder catheter went in without difficulty and promptly drained close to three liters of urine. At about the halfway draining point, a soundless sigh of relief could be noted on his previously unrevealing face. By the end, he was outwardly smiling. At this point, while I was palpating his abdomen for the presence of tenderness, he suddenly and without warning took a careful and delicate hold of my right hand with both of his, raised my hand to his face, and planted a kiss on the back of my hand, while vigorously nodding his head up and down. That was the first time in my life to have the back of my hand kissed! It was quite the surprise. My initial thought was the obvious. He was thanking me for alleviating his pain. That was simple enough. I went back to my other emergency department patients with a little bit of a smile on my face.

I returned to my home in the early morning hours after my shift ended. During that same emergency department shift, I had cared for several critically ill or injured patients, including a teenager who had fallen twenty-five feet off a roof, two high-speed motorcycle accident victims, a carbon monoxide poisoning, and a gunshot wound. Pretty serious stuff. The kind of cases for which emergency medicine physicians are trained and which we, in a black medical humor way, like to be involved. You would think, as I recapped my shift, that the dramatic, life-threatening cases would be the ones to capture my attention. They all went well, meaning the patients, though critically ill or injured, received the right diagnostic and therapeutic interventions at the right time. Time would tell if they lived or died. But my attention was not focused on the obvious. It was drawn to this seventy-nine-year-old Amharic-speaking gentleman with the urinary retention. I focused on his spontaneous action of kissing the back of my hand.

As I now recall that kiss, it was way more than just a thank-you. It was a physical show of gratitude, kindness, and love. It was a demonstration of the bond we humans have for each other, regardless of how far apart our worlds seem to be. It was a universal human action that transcended personal circumstances. We started the day as total strangers, both of us a product of cultures quite dissimilar, and finished united and linked in a permanent human bond. A stranger kissing the back of the hand of another stranger. This same action, applied across the seven billion humans walking the Earth today, would result in something truly remarkable. It is a reason to have faith and hope. It is a reason to believe that we, despite the often obvious and glaring differences, are more alike than sometimes we wish to think.

CHAPTER 27

A Giggling
Three-Year-Old Boy

A THREE-YEAR-OLD BOY WAS BROUGHT TO THE emergency department after swallowing a small toy. The little boy did not tell his mother he had swallowed something. There was no choking, gagging, or vomiting noticed by the mother. Had it not been for the fact that the toy was a small ambulance with a battery powered red light that flashed every second or two, the mother would likely have never known. In the well-lit examination room, the dim red light could barely be seen. Turn the lights off in the examination room, and it became a spectacle! There was no mistaking what this playful child had done—he had swallowed the toy ambulance! Every second or two, the red light would flash, lighting up his upper abdomen.

The emergency nurse triage notes on the chart simply stated the child had swallowed something. No mention of a flashing red-light toy ambulance. I walked into the examination room for my initial assessment. What I discovered was a three-year-old boy sitting on the gurney, with shorts and sandals on but no shirt. He was intently staring down at his abdomen, and would let out this pure, unadulterated staccato giggle of laughter that coincided with the appearance of each flash of red light. He was totally enthralled and entertained by the light display. His mother's response wavered between laughing with her child and being noticeably concerned about the possible dangers of this ingestion, particularly the ingestion of a toy with a battery. The mother had googled battery ingestions and discovered they can lead to serious complications and morbidity.

The medical aspects of this case were straightforward. A radiograph demonstrated the toy ambulance to be located within the stomach, which was consistent with where we saw the flashing red light. The battery was enclosed within the toy and did not pose as much a threat of ulceration and bowel injury as bare ingested batteries. So, the toy could be allowed to take its natural course. It would need to meander its way through several feet of small and large bowel over the following days before being passed in a bowel movement. Reassurance was provided to the mother that this was a safe strategy. The mother returned the patient to the emergency department two days later. She had been examining, indeed, dissecting, each stool carefully without finding the toy. Only a loving mother would perform this duty. A repeat radiograph demonstrated the toy ambulance to be in the distal colon, 4 inches or so from the rectal opening. It had moved a long distance and was inches away from being expelled. The mother was reassured. The child did not return to the emergency department again. The toy ambulance presumably had exited his gastrointestinal system over the ensuing days.

The captivating aspect of this case was the child's laughter. It is years later, and I can still hear it. Laughter is a physical expression of happiness. It connotes joy, bliss, pleasure, and contentment. It truly is infectious. "Laugh and the whole world laughs with you," attributed to Ella Wheeler Wilcox (November 5, 1850–October 30, 1919), who was an American author and poet. Every hospital employee who entered this child's room that day: nurse, nursing assistant, registrar, volunteer, environmental services worker—indeed everyone—giggled and laughed as freely and without inhibition as the child. Any negative mood, worldly concerns, and real-life worries were immediately and temporarily set aside and replaced with this gift of laughter. I wish I could prescribe laughter to my patients as well as self-prescribe it. I, like I suspect many adults, do not laugh often or loud enough.

Laughter is a wonderful endowment. A child's laughter is special. It is spontaneous, pure, natural, and unadulterated. Unfortunately, many times adults outgrow this special aspect of childhood. We get serious and absorbed, bogged down with lots of stuff that consumes our life. There are other changes we undergo as we progress from child to adult. Children look upon new things with total wonder and enchantment. When was the last time you saw an adult display wonder or enchantment? This brings me to one of the things that my Higher Power perhaps could have done better. Would it not be totally awesome (I am channeling my inner teenager with my word selection), if, when we turned, say sixty, instead of continuing to an old and decrepit state, we started to age reverse, go backward, and thus relive our youth again? We could apply the wisdom of old age to the beauties of our second youth. Youth would not be wasted on the young anymore. Your biologic kids would end up taking care of you as children. And their children would some-day take care of them as children. What goes around, would come around...one of several improvement sug-gestions I would make to my Higher Power.

CHAPTER 28

Nurses and Angels

THE PATIENT WAS A PREVIOUSLY HEALTHY, SIXTY-FIVE-YEAR-OLD male. He had a history of high blood pressure but otherwise did not have any other significant, ongoing health issues. One morning, while having breakfast with his wife, he suddenly became unable to speak and developed profound weakness of the right side of his body. His wife recognized the symptoms as a stroke and called 911. The paramedics, after briefly examining the patient in his kitchen, radio-called in a stroke code to the emergency department. This radio call set into motion a protocol cascade designed to ensure timely formal diagnosis of and therapy for the stroke. The most common type of stroke occurs when a blood clot forms in a brain artery. The blood clot prevents adequate blood delivery to the brain and results in the death of brain cells. The patient, now in our emergency department stabilization room, had just consented to receiving a blood-clot-dissolving medication. Although he was unable to speak or move the right side of his body, he was fully aware of his surroundings and had full comprehension of what was happening to him. He clearly understood his dire circumstance. His countenance, despite the motor deficits to his face caused by the stroke, still revealed his emotions. In one word, he was petrified. He realized his life lay in the hands of complete strangers, in a world in which he knew nothing.

I gave my nurse the order to administer a blood-clot-dissolving medication. As she acknowledged my verbal order, she noted the look on the patients face. The nurse, seeing and understanding this look without a word spoken, came to the bedside for twenty seconds. In those twenty seconds, she wiped the sweat off the patient's face, put her hand on his shoulder, and told him to believe and trust that he was in good hands. The patient's anxiety level reduced significantly, at least the visible manifestations of that anxiety. The nurse then set about the complex task of administering the blood-clot-dissolving medication. I have practiced emergency medicine for thirty-six years in an urban, academic trauma center. It is impossible to count the number of nurses I have worked with over that time period. It probably numbers in the thousands. I am simply amazed by and deeply indebted to nurses.

I am amazed because of the incredible breadth of skills and knowledge they possess. Their responsibilities are vast, providing extremely varied undertakings on a day-to-day basis. The complex tasks they perform in time-limited situations is impressive. This stroke patient provides a great example (i.e., the ability of the nurse to deliver a blood-clot-dissolving medication to a patient having a certain type of stroke). These medications need to be administered as soon as possible, because every minute that passes with decreased brain blood flow due to the blood clot means more dead brain cells and a worse outcome. It is literally a life-or-death situation, or at the very least, preventing a life with severe permanent neurologic damage. These blood-clot-dissolving medications need to be administered quickly. These medications are also dangerous, in and of themselves. They can cause bleeding, and if this bleeding occurs in the brain, it can worsen the stroke outcome, if not hasten death. Accidentally giving too much of this medication increases the chances of a bleeding complication. This medication needs to be prepared at the bedside into the correct concentration and delivered to the patient on a weight-based dose. The medication is given intravenously by two separate methods. First, a bolus is given, meaning a direct amount given rapidly over a one-minute time period, followed by an infusion whereby the rest of the medication is delivered slowly over an hour or two. The infusion is delivered with a complex, electronic infusion pump, which carefully regulates the amount of drug the patient is receiving over a specified time period. Each individual patient with a stroke gets a different bolus and infusion rate based on their weight.

The bottom line is that a potentially dangerous medication needs to be administered as quickly as possible using a complex piece of equipment, and the dose calculations change for every single individual stroke patient. This is difficult, intricate, and stress-filled work.

The physician's part of this therapy is straightforward. The physician needs to decide this medication is indicated and to order the medication be given. That's it. Physicians make the important decision to give the medication. It is up to the nurse to make it happen safely and quickly. This interaction between nurse and physician is repeated many times a day in the emergency department. Physicians place orders for medications and lab tests, but the nurses make it happen. I admire them for their almost universal "can do" attitude.

Delivering medications and performing lab tests are not the only reasons I admire nurses. They frequently spend much more time at the patient's bedside than anyone else caring for a given patient. They deliver their care in a compassionate, caring, and thoughtful manner. Although not necessarily in their job description and not technically working to the top of their license, they bathe, dress, and hold hands with their patients. They console patients and their families while providing hope and strength. Their role in the successful management and treatment of patients cannot be overemphasized. Nurses are the pillar of care in our emergency department.

I stated earlier I am also indebted to nurses. This is for several important reasons. First, I have learned a lot of medicine from nurses throughout the years. They have taught me so very much. I can clearly remember the exact moment I decided to pay careful attention to nurse clinical assessments of patients. I was a brand-new intern, as I had just graduated medical school and was in my first year of emergency medicine residency training. I had the letters "MD" after my name, but that did not translate into much knowledge and skill. "MD" after my name at that time in my career more accurately could have been an acronym for "Mostly Dumb"! I had a patient that, in the middle of the night, became unstable and critically ill. I was alone at the bedside with the patient's nurse. This nurse was extremely well respected and had twenty years of critical care experience. I remember looking up at all the monitors, which displayed numbers indicating I had an extremely ill patient with death rapidly approaching unless quick and appropriate action was taken. I must have had a bewildered, maybe even frightened look on my face, because the nurse turned to me and calmly stated "What I have seen done in this situation before is..." She proceeded to tell me what should be done for this patient. This nurse could have told me to call my senior supervisor, or even just start to do it herself under the guise that a crashing patient dictates immediate action. Instead, she calmly taught me some medicine in a way that soothed my physician ego and provided the immediate care the patient so desperately needed. Her advice was spot on. From that moment on I have made it a personal policy to pay attention to what nurses think, say, and do. As a result, I have learned an enormous amount from my nurse colleagues over the years.

The second reason I am indebted to nurses is because of the care and watchful attention they provide to my patients. They are at the bedside much more than me, the physician. I am indebted to them for noticing the subtle cues that a patient's condition is worsening, and not only making me aware of the developing clinical deterioration but making sure I was focused and reacting to that issue in a time-sensitive manner.

I am indebted to them for wiping the sweat off my scared stroke patient's forehead and taking the time to really deliver patient-centered care when my mind and thoughts were focused on the mechanics of healthcare delivery.

When I take a high-level view of the field of nursing and its relationship to the care of the ill and injured, nurses are clearly the glue that holds the healthcare system together. I admire their work, their compassion, and their selflessness. I suspect there is a special place in heaven for them. Over the years I have witnessed many patients professing their nurse to be an angel on Earth, specifically sent to them by their Higher Power.

CHAPTER 29

The Mission

THE YOUNG MALE PATIENT HAD A HISTORY of schizophrenia as well as alcohol and illicit drug abuse. He presented to the emergency department in his usual, recurrent, and difficult-to-manage condition. He was yelling, cursing, and verbally abusing anyone who came into his eyesight. Racial slurs were verbally thrown at healthcare providers of color. Profane sexual insults that would affront even the most hardened of female healthcare providers were frequent and loud. He threatened physical harm to anyone who came physically close to him. The last action this patient undertook prior to being sedated for his safety and the safety of the healthcare staff was to deliberately urinate on the floor as an act of defiance or as a proxy of his assault on those around him.

I watched this entire scenario unfold before my eyes. I observed the reactions of the healthcare workers involved in his care, and the cleanup of the mess he had made. It appeared the experienced healthcare workers were angry and the less experienced were shocked and traumatized. The most notable thing to me was that angry or stunned, all the healthcare workers went about their business in a most professional manner.

Our hospital is one of America's Essential Hospitals, a so-called safety-net hospital. Like all of America's Essential Hospitals, we champion excellence in health-care for all, regardless of the social or economic cir-cumstance of the individual patient. Such hospitals are committed to ensuring access to care and optimal health for America's most vulnerable people.

Our mission, "...to ensure access to outstanding care for everyone..." is easy to say and very hard to do. A large proportion of our patient population is socially and economically disadvantaged, many with no or mini-mal healthcare insurance. Coupled with the fact that so-cioeconomic determinants of health play a critical role in improving and maintaining health, providing care in an efficient and effective manner to our patient popu-lation is extremely challenging. It is difficult to provide adequate care for a patient with an open infected wound when the patient cannot afford antibiotics and whose homelessness precludes the ability to adequately care for the wound. Many of our patients have significant psychi-atric disease as a comorbid condition preventing their ability to recognize a worsening of their medical condi-tion. It is difficult for a homeless patient with a broken ankle to elevate and ice their injury, and it is difficult for a homeless patient with pneumonia to have bed rest. The challenges are many. The list of difficulties is endless.

Providing care to our patient population can be very problematic and challenging. The patient's lack of resources, whether it be finances, food, housing, and friends or family to help care for them, contributes to worse health outcomes. Significant psychiatric disease precludes patient understanding of their illness or injury. Social, cultural, and language barriers are all obstacles to providing outstanding and patient-centered care. Substance abuse issues with alcohol and illicit drugs often impedes timely delivery of follow-up care. Inner-city violence unfortunately adversely affects everyone involved.

For most of the seven thousand or so employees of our safety-net hospital, we do not share this daily plight in our own personal lives. We go home after our shift to our safe, comfortable, food-filled home, apartment, condo, or townhouse. Relating and interacting with our patients can be overwhelming and daunting. At times it can seem impossible to provide the care that we have been trained to deliver because of these innumerable patient support impediments. In many respects it is physically and mentally easier to work as a provider in a healthcare setting outside of an American Essential Hospital.

Yet the vast majority of our seven thousand employees work in our hospital because of the mission. They do so despite the difficulties they encounter to carry out that mission. I used to think of the personnel who carry out this mission in very narrow terms (i.e., physicians, physician assistants, nurse practitioners, nurses, and nursing assistants). I thought of serving this mission in terms of those employees who have direct patient care contact. It was a very narrow and egocentric viewpoint. The fact is that when you sit down and talk with the nonclinical employees of our hospital, they are just as dedicated to the mission as those with direct patient care contact and involvement. Employees working to provide our patients, their families and visitors, and our hospital staff healthy and enjoyable meals are dedicated to the mission. Environmental service employees are dedicated, providing the hospital with a safe, clean, and infection-free environment. So, too, for information technology, administration, bioelectronics, central processing, facilities and management, and laboratory services, to name but a few nonclinical departments that are critical for and dedicated to this mission. Most of our employees, both clinicians and nonclinicians, could find the same job and job description in a healthcare facility with less stressful conditions and more resources. These other healthcare facilities have patients that are easier to care for simply as a result of the resources the healthcare providers and their patients have available to them. Yet our employees stay at our mission-driven institution. They stay for prolonged periods of time. Many spend their entire career here.

It is this mission-driven work to care for the vulnerable that is truly noteworthy. The mission spans across seven thousand employees and includes many job classifications and pay scales. Our employees are extremely diverse, reflecting on the patient population they serve. Yet there is a very common thread woven within the foundational fabric of our institution. It is caring for the vulnerable and the less fortunate. Like gravity, this acts as a unifying force for seven thousand gifted and giving individuals. It pulls us together. When driving to work and when starting a shift, I think of this mission-driven pull. Like gravity, it allows all the employees of our institution to bond tightly, unified in a common cause.

CHAPTER 30

Blood

I SEE, TOUCH, AND SMELL BLOOD EVERY day while working in the emergency department. The volume of blood I see varies tremendously, from a small speckle or a single drop to a life-threatening torrential outpour. The color of blood is distinctly unique. Oxygen-laden arterial blood is a bright cherry red, while venous blood, relatively poor in oxygen content, has a deeper, duskier appearance. The color is so unique that "blood red" is often used as a descriptor of one shade in the seemingly limitless number of shades of the color red. Like the color of blood, the touch of blood is just as distinctive. Its viscosity and texture are unlike any other liquids. Its feel changes the longer it is exposed to air on your gloved fingers. Initially it feels just slightly more viscous than plain water, but over a relatively short period of time develops a tacky consistency, right before it dries completely. As for the smell of blood, well, I just cannot describe it. The smell must be experienced.

How humans react to the sight, feel, and smell of blood is totally dependent on the person experiencing the interaction with blood and the circumstances involved in that interaction. Some humans faint at the mere sight of blood, whether it be theirs or someone else's. Emergency physicians, after years of training and experience, are desensitized to the sight of blood. Most of the time we hardly give it a second thought. In fact, there are times where seeing blood is a welcomed site for the emergency physician, such as when the emergency physician is struggling to start an IV on a chubby one-year-old child who has no visible or palpable veins. Most times seeing blood is an expected and normal process of the pathophysiology of a given medical or trauma case. We hardly give the sight of blood any notice. For the most part, the sight of blood is a normal part of our regular daily routine. Sometimes, though, it is not. I teach our new medical students, interns, and residents what was taught to me thirty-six years ago. It is an old tongue-in-cheek mordant adage never to panic or worry about bloody hemorrhage because "all bleeding eventually stops." This adage is technically true, as bleeding stops either because the physician was able to control the hemorrhage, or it stops because the patient bled out their entire blood volume onto the floor. While this is technically true, it is not reassuring. It is hard to remain calm when a patient is trying their best to bleed to death in front of you. There is a point in every case involving major hemorrhage when, no matter how seasoned the emergency physician, the volume of blood hits a critical visual point, the point at which physician panic inevitably sets in.

There is something else I have come to understand about blood. Young or old, male or female, gay or straight, white, black, Native American or Asian, intellectually gifted or mentally challenged, conservative or liberal, rich or poor, or whatever descriptive examples you might wish to employ—all humans have at least one thing in common: our blood. After a particularly bloody case in which the patient hemorrhaged onto the cold, tiled medical floor, the color, smell, and texture of blood is all the same, regardless of the personal characteristics of that individual patient. Blood is a unifying physical human trait. It binds us together. As a physician I am aware of the racial and genetic differences in blood at the molecular level. But in my daily interaction with blood at the clinical level, well, frankly, it's all equivalent. We all bleed the same color. Throughout the ages blood has rightfully been considered the giver of life, an essential ingredient for human life. I ponder why we discriminate based on arbitrary and superficial human external traits such as skin color instead of gaining a deeper understanding and unification of the important characteristics of humans, like our blood.

Every time I see the blood mobile, a traveling unit in which volunteers donate their precious blood, establish itself near the front entrance of our hospital, I get a comforting and warm feeling. There is a steady, relentless line of humans freely donating their own priceless, life-generating blood for the purposes of helping another, unknown, stranger human being. That is how I picture blood, as a unifying human trait, a characteristic that fastens us together. I often wonder as I stare at that blood-mobile line of volunteers if the blood one of those individuals is about to donate will be used by me to help one of my patients. Or, for that matter, to help a relative, friend, or perhaps, even myself.

CHAPTER 31

Organ Donation

IT WAS AN UNFATHOMABLE AND HORRENDOUS ACCIDENT. An active three-year-old boy had been climbing up a tall, narrow television stand when the stand and the heavy, large television sitting atop tipped over toward the child. The heavy television landed squarely on the child's head. The parents, just a few steps away in an adjacent room, heard the terrible sound and ran into the family room to discover an unbearable tragedy unfolding before their eyes. The parents called 911. The intervening time between the 911 call to ambulance arrival must have seemed like an eternity to the parents. All they could do was hold their child close and press a towel on a bleeding scalp laceration. The paramedics found the child unconscious with an obvious severe head injury. The child was taken to our emergency department stabilization room and met with a large cadre of nurses and physicians who would attempt to save his life. The child was intubated, meaning a breathing tube was placed into his throat, and he was placed on a ventilator. A severe brain injury, with possible brain swelling and/or bleeding, was the likely etiology for this child's unconsciousness.

When the brain swells or there is significant brain bleeding, an increase in intracranial pressure occurs. This means the pressure within his confined skull space would be abnormally elevated, leading to a decreased blood flow to the brain, resulting in more brain injury. Several medications were given to temporarily decrease his presumed increased intracranial pressure. This would allow time to obtain a head CT scan, determine the exact nature of the brain injury, and decide whether it would be amenable to surgical correction. Unfortunately, the head CT scan demonstrated no bleeding that could be corrected by emergency surgery. The head CT scan showed diffuse, severe brain swelling and edema. The prognosis was grim. Aggressive supportive critical care, including a continuation of several medications to decrease his brain swelling, were the only treatments that could be offered. The next forty-eight hours would be crucial in determining this child's potential recovery.

Over the course of the next few days, the parents never left this child's bedside. Forty-eight hours passed during this constant parental vigil, and the child's neurologic status had only deteriorated during that time. Bedside neurologic examination, electroencephalography (a measure of brain electrical activity), and brain blood-flow measurements determined with medical imaging were unfortunately congruent and conclusive. This child had suffered irreversible brain death. At seventy-two hours postinjury, the family consented to organ donation. This child had suffered an isolated brain injury with all his other organs remaining fully intact and functional. As a result, multiple organs including lungs, heart, pancreas, and kidneys were transplanted into waiting pediatric organ recipients.

I followed this child's hospital course and was saddened to hear of his brain death. Given his initial head CT scan and presenting neurologic examination, it was the expected outcome. The emotional pain parents endure to consent to and allow for organ donation for a three-year-old child with sudden and totally unexpected traumatic brain death is hard to comprehend. The fact they were able to do this is remarkable in and of itself. Yet what sets this case apart from the many other patients (and their families) I have cared for that subsequently donated their organs is what happened four weeks later. A letter came addressed to the healthcare staff of the emergency department. It was a thank-you note from the mother and father of this three-year-old boy. The note stated that they were grateful and appreciative of the great care their little precious child had received in the emergency room. Most notably, they were especially thankful that the care rendered in the emergency room had made the ultimate gift of organ donation possible. The emergency room healthcare workers had staved off his imminent death and stabilized this patient long enough for the complex process of organ donation to be successful. The knowledge that their child's vital organs were helping other kids to live meant the world to them. When I read this thank-you note, I drew a mental picture of the mother and father sitting down at their kitchen table, writing this painful note. How incredibly brave, generous, and thoughtful an act, not only deciding on organ donation, but taking the time to let the emergency department healthcare workers know that, even though their precious child had died, they were greatly in our debt for saving their child long enough to give onto others.

CHAPTER 32

A Major Disaster

I WAS DRIVING HOME FROM WORK. IT was a beautiful, hot summer day, and as such it had been a busy day in the emergency department. I was tired and still a little tense from a couple of difficult critical cases I had encountered earlier that day. As I have often done during my career as an emergency physician, I used the forty-minute commute home to begin to relax and unwind from whatever stressors I had encountered during my shift.

Today's commute unwinding was interrupted after only ten minutes of driving. My pager made its loud, obnoxious, painfully interrupting and irritating sound. The digital text message was clear and direct. An Orange Alert had been initiated. This alert is only called when a major disaster has occurred with the possibility of many critical patients presenting to our hospital. This alert is generated when the number of causalities is expected to exceed normal daily operational resources. Despite twice-per-year practice drills, this was the first time in my career that a real Orange Alert disaster had been activated. All available hospital employees were to report immediately to the hospital. For me, that meant turning around and heading straight back to the emergency department. I quickly turned on the radio hoping the news agencies had picked up on their scanners the nature of this disaster.

A local radio station soon provided me the information. A bridge of a major highway had collapsed into the river below. This bridge was eight lanes across and averaged 140,000 vehicle crossings per day. Its highest point was 115 feet above the river. It was rush hour, and traffic going over the bridge had been bumper to bumper. Investigation after the event revealed there were 111 vehicles involved in the collapse. The bridge, located in the downtown area, was less than two miles from our level 1 trauma medical center. We would be getting critically injured patients very quickly. The only question was: How many patients?

I arrived at the hospital and ran down several hallways with my destination being the emergency department stabilization room. Up to four critically injured patients can receive lifesaving care in this one particularly large, well-designed, and thoroughly equipped room. However, this room will not be big enough. We would likely be needing to care for critically injured patients in other areas of the emergency department. Running down these hospital hallways was like running through a thick human maze of healthcare workers. The hospital was abuzz with activity. Hospital employees of all job classifications were going each way in the hallways and hallway intersections, busily preparing for their role in the unfolding catastrophe. Physicians, nurses, advanced practice providers, phlebotomists, pharmacists, nursing assistants, lab and medical imaging technicians, social workers, health unit coordinators, physical and occupational therapists, environmental service workers, and chaplains were scurrying to their respective assignments. It did not matter if you normally worked the day, evening, or night shift. If you received the Orange Alert signal, you reported for duty.

To an outsider, it was pure, unadulterated chaos. To me, it was organized chaos. I was appropriately nervous about what might be unfolding before my eyes. But I was confident that our department would perform well. We had trained for this very moment.

I reached the emergency department stabilization room and was immediately assigned to be the leader of one of the four beds. I had a team of three nurses, several interns and resident physicians in training, a respiratory therapist, and two nursing assistants. We were ready. I looked around the room, and each of the other three beds had similar teams, standing in place, simply waiting. On the periphery of this large room was an entire circle of perhaps fifty support staff, waiting to assist in any manner deemed necessary. This included refreshing and restocking medical supplies and medications, transporting patients to medical imaging or the operating room, and cleaning the bed and floor after each case. Not more than a few minutes later, the first of the critically injured patients arrived by ambulance. My first patient was, indeed, critically ill with a severe penetrating

chest injury. My first thought when I laid eyes on this patient caused a split second of hesitation. *If the injuries on
this patient are any indication, this is going to be a very long
night.* I had no idea how many patients we would be getting. After allowing myself that brief distracting thought,
we quickly got to work on our first patient.

As it turns out, twenty-three critically injured patients presented to our emergency department in the
next ninety minutes. It was organized chaos, and it
worked. All patients received excellent and timely care.
I remember sitting down in a quiet corner of the emergency department after the last critical patient had been
admitted to the hospital, processing what had just occurred. Although the emergency department had quiet-
ed down, with no new critically injured patients arriving,
the hospital was alive with activity. The operating room
and radiology suites were packed and busy. I took the
time to meditate and visually imagined the thousands
of individuals involved in this tragedy. I pictured the victims. Young and old, male and female, and members of
diverse racial and ethnic backgrounds. These patients
simply were in the wrong place at the wrong time. Call it
their fate, destiny or just bad luck.

I also imagined the immediate nonprofessional by-
standers who had risked personal injury and jumped at
the opportunity to rescue those patients at the scene.
Those Good Samaritans who pulled victims out of their
precariously dangling or crushed cars. School children
were rescued off a school bus that was dangerously close
to falling into the river one hundred feet below. The

police and fire rescue personnel, who put their own lives in danger by climbing down the pile of unstable cement, wading or jumping into the river, looking for and finding survivors, and pulling them to safety. Finally, I thought of all the hospital staff working feverishly in diverse jobs they have been uniquely trained to perform.

I had an intense feeling of belonging, not just as a member of the hospital staff, but as a member of the human species. I worked that day with friends, well-known coworkers, and complete strangers. We were all there for the same reason: to help fellow human beings through this heartbreaking tragedy. The resulting personal emotional feeling for me was poignant. It reaffirmed for me just how fragile life is, and how, in an instant, our lives can be changed forever. It confirmed that helping is a natural human instinct, given to us by a Higher Power. We can help in a major, mass-casualty disaster that is witnessed by millions of people via worldwide telecommunications, and we can surreptitiously and inconspicuously help by giving our seat up to a frail-appearing senior citizen standing on a transit bus.

CHAPTER 33

A Cold Winter Morning

A CAR CARRYING FIVE CHILDREN SKIDDED OFF a highway entrance ramp, tumbled down an embankment, and completely submerged in icy water in January. The accident occurred during morning rush hour and was witnessed by passengers in nearby cars, who promptly notified 911. A robust prehospital response including police, fire, ambulance services, and SCUBA diving rescue personnel, was quickly generated. One by one the rescue divers pulled the individual kids out of the submerged car. Each child was severely hypothermic (cold body temperature) and in cardiac arrest, meaning their heart was not beating, and they were not breathing. Each child was placed into a waiting ambulance undergoing basic manual CPR and transported to our emergency department.

Treatment of hypothermic cardiac arrest victims is extremely complex, especially in children. The immediate goal is to provide cardiovascular support while rewarming the patient. This requires a significant amount of advanced medical equipment, supplies, and healthcare personnel. Providing cardiovascular support to a patient with a cold, nonbeating heart is difficult and can be accomplished by several different methods. These methods include basic manual CPR, CPR using an automated mechanical plunger device, and internal heart CPR after a large incision into the chest has been made enabling the physician to squeeze the heart directly with their hand.

Cardiac bypass or extracorporeal membrane oxygenation are two advanced and complex methods that can be utilized to treat patients in hypothermic cardiac arrest, but are resource-intense and require special equipment for pediatric patients to which our hospital did not have direct access. These two methods entail placing a large catheter (tube) into a large artery and vein, and the patient's blood is circulated by pump through an oxygenator and heater. The warmed, oxygen-saturated blood is then delivered back to the patient with enough pressure to circulate throughout the patient's body.

Hypothermia, somewhat paradoxically, protects the brain from injury related to lack of blood flow with resultant deprivation of oxygen and glucose (sugar). Brain cells, when made sufficiently cold, require markedly reduced amounts of oxygen and glucose to survive, creating a protective environment. This is because the metabolism of the brain cells is slowed considerably when cold. The medical literature is replete with articles detailing miraculous neurologic recovery in patients with prolonged cardiac arrest related to submersion in icy water. In fact, the longest documented submersion time with meaningful neurologic survival is eighty-three minutes!

As a result of these miracle cases, there is an axiom in medicine that when treating a hypothermic cardiac arrest victim, "a patient is not dead until they are warm and dead." These five pediatric patients needed aggressive care and definitive rewarming before any proclamation of death. This would take many, many hours to accomplish.

One pediatric hypothermic cardiac arrested patient is difficult to treat. Five such patients, all arriving at virtually the same time, quickly overwhelm resources. No practice disaster scenarios mimicking this situation had ever been performed at our institution. Innovation and quick, on-your-feet, commonsense decision-making was going to be important.

All five patients presented with ongoing manual CPR by rescuers. Automated, mechanical plunger CPR devices, which deliver superior chest compressions when compared to manual CPR, are designed for adults, not small children. As a result, these five patients all needed manual CPR, and they were going to need it for a prolonged time period. It takes a significant amount of time to rewarm a severely hypothermic patient. A call went out to the entire hospital staff that help was needed in the emergency department. What occurred next is the memorable and extraordinary part of this event. Healthcare personnel—physicians, nurses, nursing assistants, indeed, anyone available who had basic CPR training and skills—reported to the emergency department. Lines of CPR volunteers were formed. There are four beds in our critical care room, and the newly found CPR volunteers formed a long line that was perpendicular to each bedside. When the person performing manual compressions became tired, they handed the CPR job to the next person in line, and the just-finished CPR volunteer went to the back of the line, recovering from their CPR exertion and awaited yet another turn. As the minutes and hours progressed, present CPR volunteers who had other clinical care obligations were replaced by new CPR recruits. It was a surreal scene that could not have been previously imagined. Predicting which, if any, of these children would survive was impossible. Their care consisted of CPR, ventilation, and aggressive rewarming. This prolonged care lasted for hours and hours. A multitude of CPR volunteers, each working until they were exhausted, repeated the process again and again, until life or death proclaimed itself in these young victims.

Of the five children, three of them lived, all with good neurologic outcomes. They would not have lived save for the tireless efforts of nameless CPR volunteers.

Enjoying Life

AN EIGHTEEN-YEAR-OLD GIRL PRESENTED CRITICALLY ILL TO the emergency department. She started vomiting bright red blood when she first woke up during the early morning hours in her college dorm room. The frightful, blood-filled vomiting continued for several hours, worsening in its volume and frequency. It did not take long before the amount of blood lost reached a critical volume, at which time her blood pressure plummeted, and her heart rate soared. This was accompanied by profound dizziness and a couple episodes of fainting when she tried to stand up and go to the bathroom. Sensing something terrible was happening, she dialed 911 from her cell phone, and promptly laid down on the bathroom floor to await ambulance arrival.

The paramedics entered her dorm room to find her semiconscious on the floor in a large pool of blood that clearly was originating from her mouth. The patient was quickly loaded onto a stretcher, placed in the ambulance, and transferred with lights flashing and sirens blasting. Vehicles ahead of the speeding ambulance, hearing the sirens and seeing the flashing lights, separated to both sides of the road, creating a narrow path and enabling the ambulance to circumvent morning rush-hour traffic.

When the patient arrived in the emergency department critical care room, the first thing I noticed beyond her markedly decreased level of consciousness was the deathly, ghost-white color of her skin. Describing her skin as pale was clearly an understatement. Bedroom sheets had more color than her face. This patient had lost a significant amount of blood. Her blood pressure was perilously low, and her heart pounded at a dangerously fast rate of 180 beats per minute to compensate for the acute blood loss.

The patient was continuing to vomit blood, and because of her decreased level of consciousness, she was in danger of choking and literally drowning in her own blood. As a result, the patient was quickly sedated and chemically paralyzed, and a breathing tube placed into her trachea (throat). She was placed on the ventilator. Multiple large-bore intravenous catheters were placed in small, superficial arm veins, as well as into large, deep neck and groin veins. Her initial hemoglobin, a measure of how much blood a person has, was 33 percent of the normal value. Blood transfusions were rapidly instituted. Medications were infused to increase her blood pressure, as well as slow down the rate of gastrointestinal bleeding. A very large diameter gastric tube was inserted into her mouth and fed down into her stomach. Up through this gastric tube came fresh, bright red blood. The blood had to be coming from a ruptured arterial blood vessel in her esophagus or stomach. The possible etiologies for the blood vessel rupture were many, but high on the potential list included a gastric stomach ulcer. Up to this point in her life, her health had always been perfect, and there was no history of alcohol abuse, which can lead via several mechanisms to severe upper gastrointestinal hemorrhage. After becoming relatively stable in the emergency department, she was transported to the medical intensive care unit.

Over the next twenty-four hours, her course was rocky and uncertain. She continued to bleed intermittently, and she required blood transfusions and powerful medications to maintain an adequate blood pressure and stave off shock. She remained sedated and on a ventilator, completely unaware of her surroundings and plight. She underwent endoscopy, where a lighted camera on a flexible cord was inserted through her mouth and advanced through her esophagus and into her stomach to visualize the focus of bleeding. A stomach ulcer that had eroded into a main stomach artery turned out to be the culprit. Various procedures using this lighted flexible fiberoptic scope were successful in stopping the hemorrhage at the exact point of bleeding. The patient's medical condition stabilized.

I went up to the medical intensive care unit the following afternoon to see how she was progressing. The infused medications used to support her blood pressure had been weaned to a lower rate, and she had stopped requiring blood transfusions. I arrived shortly after her sedative infusion was halted, and I decided to remain in the intensive care unit to see how she responded. I was standing at the foot of her bed reading her medical chart. The sedative medication quickly wore off, and within twenty minutes the patient opened her eyes and began to look around the room. Her eyes had a terrified "what happened and where the hell am I" look. I pulled up a chair and started conversing with her. Although she could not speak as the breathing tube was still down her throat, I verbally answered her unspoken question. She then signaled for a piece of paper on which to write. Her first written statement was a question. Mind you, she is still on a ventilator, receiving powerful supportive blood pressure elevating medications intravenously and remains critically ill. At first her written question did not register any meaning with me, mostly because its context was so incongruous to her current predicament. She simply wrote "Did I miss Dallas?" I must have had a clearly perplexed look on my face, because she then quickly scribbled, "the TV show!" At the time of this event, the highly rated TV show "Dallas" was in its national heyday and was followed weekly by millions of fans.

Are you kidding me? You almost die by hemorrhaging your entire blood volume out of your mouth, and your first thought and concern upon awakening is whether you missed a TV show? After I told her the current date and time, she seemed relieved that indeed, she had not missed the latest episode. After spending a few more minutes answering other, more relevant questions, I walked away thinking, well, that was weird! For years thereafter, I thought this eighteen-year-old was either crazy, immature, or just not in touch with reality. Her clinical condition and life-threatening dilemma did not seem to register with her at all. How could anyone think about a meaningless TV show upon awakening critically ill from a life-threatening hemorrhaging event, one in which a large percentage of your blood volume came flying out of your mouth?

Looking back on this event, I can now take a different, albeit gentler and more understanding tact. It was clear that she loved the TV show, *Dallas*. It made her smile and made her enjoy life. I have no idea if there were other things in her life that made her smile and appreciate life. Perhaps *Dallas* was the one and only. The important thing is that she had at least one thing in her life that made her beam, elevated her mood, and gave her something to look forward to and delight in. I think our Higher Power wants us to smile and enjoy life. It is why we even have the facial capacity to elicit a smile, and the ability to experience enjoyment. We don't need to be hedonistic, decadent, and constantly self-indulging, but we do have a need to appreciate some of the pleasant and rewarding things that life has to offer. It is a part of being human. A very important part of being human. So whether it is watching a TV show, playing with your grandchildren, golfing, petting your dog, gardening, watching your favorite sports team, or reading a good book, we humans need to stop and enjoy life. Our Higher Power gave us the emotion we call enjoyment. We should enjoy life as often as we can, even if it means doing so from a medical intensive-care bed, where this fun-loving teenager watched the next episode of *Dallas* the following evening.

CHAPTER 35

A Breed Apart

IT WAS LATE AT NIGHT. FROM THEIR squad car, two city police officers saw a man with an unsteady gait walking in the middle of a street with cars briskly passing on either side of him. The police car pulled alongside him, and the first thing the officers noted was the patient having an almost incoherent conversation with himself. Concerned for his safety, the police officers gathered him into their squad car with the intent of taking him to the emergency department for evaluation. When questioned by the police if he had been drinking alcohol, the man replied no, but confessed to having smoked a marijuana joint laced with phencyclidine, otherwise known as PCP. PCP is a psychoactive drug that can cause hallucinations and very erratic, sometimes violent behavior.

The patient was cooperative and calm during the police transport to the emergency department. Our emergency department has an isolated area designed to care for patients under the influence of alcohol or drugs who do not appear to be medically ill and are not in need of immediate medical care as a result of their intoxicating drug. Once there, the city police officers were met by two hospital security protection officers and a nurse. The patient remained tranquil and was taken by two hospital security protection officers and the nurse into a four-walled exam room that had a single emergency department gurney and nothing else. These rooms have no equipment, phones, or anything else that could be used as a weapon to hurt oneself or others. The city police officers then left the emergency department.

As the patient had remained quiet and compliant, he was guided onto the gurney with side rails elevated, and the nurse and the two hospital security protection officers left the exam room. The nurse went to the nurses' station, just a few feet from the door of this patient's examination room. The security officers moved a little further away to check on another patient at the other end of this secluded emergency department area.

Suddenly, there was an extremely loud crash that emanated from the recently placed patient's examination room. Fearing the patient had fallen off the bed, the nurse bolted from her chair and rushed into the room. Her first observation was that the emergency department gurney, upon which the patient had been laying, had apparently been thrown forcibly into the air and was now laying on its side against the wall. The patient had not fallen off the bed, but instead had gotten off the gurney, and in a fit of rage had tossed the heavy gurney onto its side. A split second later, out of her peripheral vision, she caught a glimpse of the patient, now charging toward her. Unfortunately, all she had was a glimpse, and there was no time for her to react and protect herself. She was punched full force in the face and knocked violently backward onto the floor.

Hearing the intense commotion, it took the two hospital security protection officers another four to five seconds after the nurse was punched to reach the exam room. The patient was standing in a threatening manner over the now sprawled out and stunned nurse. Upon seeing the security officers, the severely agitated and violent patient changed his focus and direction of attack and lunged at the two officers. A dramatic physical encounter ensued, resulting in one of the officers discharging an electroshock weapon in order to take control of this dangerous situation. It took another three officers, now a total of five, to subdue and restrain this patient.

The patient was in a state of excited delirium. This is a clinical condition that is extremely dangerous for the patient, as well as for the healthcare providers. It results in a high fever, acidosis (blood pH much lower than the normal 7.4), and destruction of muscle cells that can lead to kidney failure and sudden death from cardiac arrhythmias. Excited delirium, unfortunately, is seen frequently because of illicit substance abuse, such as methamphetamine, cocaine, PCP, and LSD. It is dramatic and it is life-threatening. Accordingly, this patient was emergently taken to the emergency department critical care room (stabilization room) for aggressive clinical management of his condition.

The assaulted nurse slowly rose to her knees, and then to her feet. She had not suffered a loss of consciousness, but it was clear she was shocked and dazed. She was visibly emotionally upset, crying and trembling ever so slightly. Her face was bruised. One of the emergency physicians promptly came to her side and walked her to a nearby unoccupied gurney to be examined.

At that very moment, literally just a minute or two after her attack, the overhead emergency department speakers announced the arrival of an ambulance transporting a patient critically injured in a motor vehicle crash. This assaulted nurse, not yet recovered from her ordeal, was responsible to cover the critical care area in the event of a second critically ill or injured patient. As the patient who had attacked her was just taken to the critical care room, this newly arriving ambulance would thus be placing a second critically ill patient in the stabilization room in a matter of a few minutes. The crash victim would be the assaulted nurse's patient.

The assaulted nurse, upon hearing the overhead announcement of a second critically ill patient, suddenly straightened her spine and posture to an upright sitting position, wiped her tears away, held her head high and shoulders back, and nodded to her examining physician, without saying a word. It was as though this assaulted and injured nurse was in a boxing match, and had just got up off the floor mat from a vicious punch, nodded to the fight referee that she was conscious, of sound mind and body, and was ready, able, and willing to continue with the fight. Her examining physician, correctly interpreting the assaulted nurse's body posture and movements, quickly told her, "No, no you don't. Let another nurse handle this second critical case. You need to rest!" Her response was simple and unequivocal. "I am going to go do my job." With that, she got up off the gurney with authority, walked down the hallway to the critical care room, swung open the doors, and proceeded to do her job.

And do her job, she did. She was at the bedside of this second critically ill patient. Her attacker, in plain view just a few feet away, was now completely subdued with strong sedative medications. This second critically injured patient demanded all her professional attention. Intravenous catheters needed to be rapidly inserted, and an assortment of lifesaving medications were rapidly administered. She performed beautifully. It was as though her attack had never happened, at least for the duration of her care of the second critically ill patient. Why did she do this? Was she stubborn and obstinate, or trying to prove her mental and physical toughness? Was this some sort of masochistic response? Did she have a concussion and was not thinking clearly? Few individuals would have been capable of responding in this manner.

As I think back on this event, I believe that her actions were driven by pure altruism, a sense of obligation, and a feeling of loyalty. The loyalty was not only directed to this critically ill patient whose life depended on her skills but extended to her coworkers. You can pick your descriptor of her actions. Selfless, self-sacrificing, humanitarian, responsible, committed, compassionate...they all describe this brave and noble healthcare professional.

CHAPTER 36

Closing Thoughts

IN THE PREPARATION AND WRITING OF THIS book, I spent many hours introspectively searching my memory for events and interactions I had with patients and their families over my thirty-six-year career. I considered which events might lend personal credence to my newfound faith. This systematic reflection can best be described as powerful, enlightening, and awakening.

As I remembered these patient cases and wrote the narratives in this book, there were patterns of thought and action that clearly arose. These patterns were intricately woven into each narrative. Recognition of these patterns led to pensive contemplation on the big questions in life. Namely, why I am here, what is my purpose in life, and why are our collective lives filled with what we construe to be good and bad events? Analyzing these patterns and attempting to answer these big life questions for myself led to these closing thoughts.

I remembered patients with grit, determination, endless hope, abounding love of life, and unrelenting humor despite their bleak circumstances. I recalled the families and friends of patients displaying unconditional love, rock-solid support, and incredible courage as they steadfastly took on and absorbed the mental anguish of being with a loved one who was suffering. The collective takeaway message for me was a deepening appreciation of human resilience.

I recollected healthcare workers (i.e., physicians, nurses, advanced practice providers, and nursing assistants) who personally and emotionally struggled shoulder to shoulder with their patients to provide care that at times was painful and frightening with unpredictable outcomes. The take-home message for me was a strong admiration of the innate human need to care for one another.

As an emergency physician practicing in an urban, level 1 trauma center, I experienced and witnessed first-hand the entire spectrum of both human emotion and human suffering. Every patient case fell somewhere on the human emotional continuum for the patient, their family, and for the healthcare workers involved. Each patient case caused elation or despair or somewhere in between those two opposite emotions.

There is a common belief that better decisions are made and better care is given by physicians who are not emotionally invested in their patients. This would seem to be particularly true during emergencies where seconds to minutes of decision-making and procedural intervention can be the difference between life and death. While this is true to some extent, namely, you do not want your physician's hands to be trembling out of emotional fear during an invasive bodily procedure, you also do not want your physician to be so emotionally detached that they really do not care about you as a person and human being. No matter how indifferent, logical, dispassionate, calm, unemotional, or detached an emergency physician might be in caring for patients and their families with acute medical and surgical emergencies, we are, nonetheless, deeply affected. A fine balance must be achieved between compassion or empathy and dissociation or separation. The fact of the matter is that we simply are invested. We can never completely divest ourselves emotionally from our patients. There is no way around it. Nor should there be. Physicians need to emotionally care for their patients in order to provide great medical care. Physicians need to be empathetic and compassionate if they want the best outcomes for their patients.

Patients come in all ages, races, body morphologies, and both genders with varied medical and surgical problems. In fact, each patient, coupled with a finite and discreet presentation to a given, individual physician, represents a distinctly unique event. No two events are alike. Events may be similar, but they are never identical. Some of our patients develop their medical and surgical problems because of their behavior. For example, if you drive a motorcycle at ninety miles per hour in the middle of the night while intoxicated with alcohol, it is not surprising that a totally preventable crash and subsequent injuries or death occurred as a result. It is tempting to blame this tragedy on the patient. This sort of tragedy is easier for an emergency physician to emotionally handle compared to, say, a three-year-old who presents critically ill and dies from acute leukemia. This innocent three-year-old patient developed a fatal disease without any self-destructive, inciting behavior. They appear to be an innocent bystander suffering tremendously without any way of controlling the circumstances that resulted in the development of their disease. Who or what do we blame for this? In the past, I blamed God. Later, I blamed the absence of a God.

Emergency physicians see the entire socioeconomic spectrum, from the homeless and destitute to the affluent and wealthy. We see the entire spectrum of health, from those individuals who have been essentially disease-free their entire lives and have never even been prescribed any medications, to those individuals suffering from innumerable diseases and taking dozens of different medications. Individuals who end up at either end of the socioeconomic and health-illness spectrums do so either as a result of their deliberate life choices, decisions, and actions, or by the result of fate, genetics, and circumstances completely out of their personal control. Often, it is a combination of the two.

For many years, I examined whatever human illness presented to me in terms of cause and effect. Smoking causes lung cancer. Driving a motorcycle while intoxicated leads to crashes. Eating too much causes obesity, and along with obesity, an almost endless list of diseases. It is part of the training of a physician. Look for the cause (i.e., the etiology), and you might have a treatment regimen or preventative measure to enact. The problem for me came after I identified the cause. The natural human instinct, after a cause is discovered, is to assign blame or responsibility.

Assigning culpability as to the cause of a clinical problem is fraught with problems for a physician. Compassion and empathy are easily lost in the blameworthiness. This personal journey was an important one for me to take as a physician. I had to find a way to reconcile the relationship between illness and injury and their causes without impugning the patient. There are cases where illness or injury are directly related to deliberate and controllable deeds on the part of the patient. Assailing the patient with blame is the easiest, but in the long run, least productive approach. It harms both the patient and the physician. In a figurative sense, it drives a harmful stake in the physician-patient relationship. Resolving this conflict that arises when patients' actions lead to untoward illness and injury and the subsequent placement of blame was difficult for me.

Resolution of this conflict between patient hardship and blame led me to develop a better, more positive, and useful personal philosophy. It can be summed up in nine words. These nine words have enabled me to mature as a physician and human being. These nine words have helped me understand human behavior and its consequences. They have made me more empathetic. What are those nine words?

"Save but for the grace of God go I."

It is a saying that has been around a long time. The phrase is reported to have been first spoken by the English evangelical preacher and martyr, John Bradford (circa 1510–1555).[3] He is said to have uttered the variant of the expression, "There but for the grace of God, goes John Bradford," when seeing criminals being led to the scaffold. It is a saying that I had thought about relatively often during my career when seeing patients that were dealt a tough hand of life to play. But I had, at least in my mind, substituted the word Luck for God. It was just bad Luck for some people to have suffered untimely tragedy or illness. The word God, for most of my life, was not a part of this saying in any meaningful way. But whether I used the word Luck or God, it meant the same thing, and had the same connotation. Any person, given the right circumstances, is perfectly capable of ending up on the wrong end of illness or injury. Any person, given the right circumstances, can make mistakes. Any person, given the right circumstances, can make the wrong decision and perform the wrong action that results in tragedy. This is not to diminish the role of personal responsibility in making correct decisions and performing correct and appropriate actions. It merely is a philosophy that accepts the flawed human condition. It is a philosophy that allows disagreement with a decision or action but allows for understanding as to how someone might make an incorrect decision given the circumstances at hand. That someone includes both you and me. This philosophy has helped me to be more tolerant. It does not assign blame, but it also does not abdicate personal

---

3 https://en.wikipedia.org/wiki/John_Bradford

responsibility. Indoctrinating this philosophy has greatly improved my ability to care for my patients without judgment. It has made me a better physician and person.

I am so grateful for that sunrise on the morning of my cardiac catheterization! I truly believe it was a sign. However, for those readers who might not believe it was a sign sent by my Higher Power, but rather believe it was just circumstance and coincidence: no worries; you are entitled to think this way! That sunrise, nonetheless, functioned as the stimulus for my personal awakening. It allowed me to relive some profound and difficult professional and personal experiences in a new light. It allowed me to view humanity and all its imperfections in a more accepting and empathetic manner.

Most importantly, as a result of this deeply personal introspection, I contemplated my role on this Earth. Through each of the encounters depicted in this book and the thousands of other patient-physician contacts I experienced that are not described in this book, I discovered that these encounters and experiences occurred for a reason. I was present for these events for a purpose, even if at the time of these events I was sleep walking through life, not cognizant or self-aware of my value or meaning in any of these events. It became clear to me that my role in this life as a physician, husband, father, and friend was to live a life in such a manner that I leave the world upon my death a little better off than I found it at my birth.

I have never been one for formal prayer, either before or after the personal events described in this book.

But a sentence in the Lord's Prayer has attracted my attention as it relates to this concept of leaving the world at the time of your death a little better off than you found it at the time of your birth. "Our Father, who art in heaven, hallowed be thy name. Thy kingdom come, thy will be done, on earth as it is in heaven." The prayer, as verbalized by a man (woman), is wishing for the perfection of our Higher Power's kingdom (i.e., heaven) to come and exist here on Earth. Perfection in this sense can be loosely described as all that is thought to be inherently good: love, compassion, charity, forgiveness, and peace; and the lack of all that is inherently bad: hate, cruelty, inhumanity, blame, and war. The purpose of all past, present, and future human interaction (i.e., the purpose of our life) is to make Earth like heaven. We strive through an infinity of human interactions to bring love, compassion, charity, forgiveness, and peace to this world. We do this slowly but inexorably. We have been doing this since humans first inhabited the Earth millions of years ago.

As I reflect on the interactions with my patients and their families described in this book, I realize that these patients, their families, and the healthcare workers who cared for them were also doing their part in leaving this world a little better off than they found it at their birth. It is easy to envision how the senior resident who gave his warm, expensive winter gloves to a homeless man is an act that will improve the world in a small but definitive way. Likewise, the landlord who gives of his time and energy in looking over his flock of elderly and vulnerable tenants. Or the mother and father of the young patient who died from accidental head trauma and made the painful decision to donate his organs. Yes, it is easy to see how these individuals contributed to an improved world. But how about the three patients in these same scenarios? How does an intoxicated, homeless man without winter gloves contribute to the betterment of society and the world? Or the elderly female patient who fell and sustained a hip fracture and was rescued by her landlord? Or the three-year-old child whose head was crushed by a heavy television, resulting in his death? Did these patients contribute? If so, how do these patients contribute as a result of their involvement? It would appear, for example, that the intoxicated, homeless, and frequently agitated man who lets punches fly at healthcare providers is NOT contributing in a positive fashion. The elderly female patient with a hip fracture and the three-year-old with the tragic life-ending accident appear to be victims of declining health and heartbreaking circumstances, respectively. How do these victims of circumstance donate and contribute to the advancement of the world? It appears that these individuals are unlucky and unfortunate people. Is this interaction one sided? Is it just the mother and father of the three-year-old who died from accidental trauma who undertook the opportunity to make this world a better place by organ donation, or does the three-year-old organ donor himself somehow contribute?

I have come to believe that indeed, the victims in these terrible events are contributing. Their tragic life events create the opportunity and circumstances that enable others to improve upon the world. These victims, while not deliberately, willingly, or consciously suffering in order to create opportunity for others, nonetheless are still creating that opportunity. In the grand scheme, defined by however the reader would like to define "A Grand Scheme," their plight empowers others around them to rise to the occasion and to contribute. When looking at this in a broader context, every human interaction and every human event is seen as an opportunity for advancement. This enables one to look upon tragic events in a new light. It has enabled me to make sense of when and why bad things happen to good people. When tragedy seemingly indiscriminately strikes a person with no overt rhyme or reason, that circumstance, that event, is creating opportunity for others. When looked at in this manner, it is not depressing. It no longer causes me to wonder why a Higher Power would allow such events, and it does not cause me to lose my faith. Rather, it is para-doxically uplifting. It serves as a positive reminder that there is good in every event. Untoward events may, at a first superficial glance, look simply horrible, but when something good happens as a result of that event, it turns into something noteworthy and great.

This reasoning can be taken a step further. It is pos-sible that in the eyes of a Higher Power, the victims of un-fortunate life episodes might indeed be the heroes, the ones looked up to, the ones gathering adulation. After all, it is the tragic events of the sufferers that enabled oth-ers to rise to the occasion, to produce acts of goodness, and to move this world to a better condition. Sufferers might very well have a special, elevated, and honored status in the afterlife!

This gets even a little more complicated. A given individual can take on the two different roles at various times during their lifetime. In one instance, an individual may be the person who, by their actions, helps another person and improves upon this imperfect world. That same Good Samaritan, so to speak, at another point in their life may be the person who needs the help and receives assistance and comfort in the form of a loving and kind act. In fact, during a lifetime, each one of us probably flips back and forth between these roles countless number of times. Those individuals whose life circumstances place them as a sufferer for their entire life are probably the rock stars in heaven, garnering utmost respect, admiration, and praise. These individuals, through their suffering, served an earthly lifetime enabling others to enhance and improve upon the human condition.

This has been a paradigm shift for me. Lest I confuse you, I still feel awful when confronted with a horrible event. I still wish it had not occurred, and I feel tremendous empathy and sympathy for the sufferer and their family. But I have stopped asking why this happened. It is a question that I cannot adequately and assuredly answer. It is a question that has been a source of past sadness and hopelessness during my professional career. I now pay more attention to the words and actions of those individuals, namely the family, friends, and healthcare workers involved in the tragedy. What good has come of this event? How has this event advanced the betterment of the world? Where is the silver lining? Taking this different tack has lifted a heavy burden. It is sunshine dissipating the fog. It sheds a new light and provides for positivity and optimism, even in the darkest of events. Instead of an overwhelming sense of despair and sorrow for the sufferer, I can almost say "thank you" to them. When I look for and find the good that comes of a tragedy, I can say "thank you" to those sufferers for giving us the opportunity to become better human beings. I can say "thank you" for advancing life on Earth closer to the perfection of life in heaven.

I have faith.

Acknowledgments

I WROTE THIS BOOK IN SECRET SILENCE. It started as a simple and short statement. A self-proclamation that, yes, as a result of an unforeseen constellation of very personal events, I believed in a Higher Power. After years of doubt followed by denial, I was able to clandestinely and somewhat fearfully admit that I believed. My first inclination in how to share this book was the idea of a posthumous revelation. Upon my death I would surprise my surviving wife and children with this book. It was never intended to be shared publicly, at least while I remained alive. It was private and personal.

In a fleeting moment of courage or recklessness, I decided to share this book with my wife, Marian, and my closest friends, Steve and Suzie Bennett. In my heart, I did not think this was a story worth telling. I was afraid it would be viewed as trite, unsophisticated, and pedestrian.

Without so much as a moment of hesitation, all three strongly encouraged me to publish. They believed in this book, more so than I. Without their faith in me, and in their own Higher Power, this book would still be in a locked, fireproof safe, next to my last will and testament. Thank you for your support, reassurance, understanding, and most importantly, your friendship.

Made in the USA
Monee, IL
13 March 2020